A Black Man's Worth!
Conqueror and Head of Household

Other Great Books by Dr. Dwayne L. Buckingham

A Black Woman's Worth: My Queen and Backbone

Qualified, yet Single: Why Good Men Remain Single

Can Black Women Achieve Marital Satisfaction? How Childhood Nurturing Experiences Impact Marital Happiness.

Unconditional Love: What Every Woman and Man Desires In A Relationship

Ground-Breaking Films by Dr. Dwayne L. Buckingham

A Black Man's Worth: Conqueror and Head of Household

A Black Woman's Worth: My Queen and Backbone

Qualified, yet Single: Why Good Men Remain Single

www.realhorizonsdlb.com

A Black Man's Worth!
Conqueror and Head of Household

How To Conquer Internalized Oppression

Dr. Dwayne L. Buckingham, LCSW, BCD

R.E.A.L. Horizons Consulting Service, LLC
Silver Spring, Maryland

A Black Man's Worth!
Conqueror and Head of Household

Unless otherwise indicated, all scripture quotations are taken from the King James Version of the Bible. In addition, any information about Black history was taken from the Wikipedia, The Free Encyclopedia.

Additional copies of this book can be purchased on-line at www.realhorizonsdlb.com or by contacting:

R.E.A.L. Horizons Consulting Service, LLC
P.O. Box 2665
Silver Spring, MD 20915
240-242-4087 Voice mail

Expanding Horizons by keeping it "R.E.A.L."

SECOND EDITION

Cover designed by Stephen Fortune

Library of Congress Control Number: 2011962622

ISBN: 978-0-9849423-0-5

For Worldwide Distribution

Printed in the United States of America

Dedication

To My Lord Jesus Christ, who protects and
nurtures me daily.

To Father Richard Chiles, my God sent father!

And

To my three brothers:
David, Elisha and Dan.

Thanks for the brotherhood, support, and motivation. I wrote
the poem on the next page to inspire you to look up when
you are feeling down.

I Can!

I can accomplish whatever I put my mind to if I believe

– I can!

Life will challenge me, but I will succeed because

– I can!

Others may influence my destiny, but I determine it because

– I can!

When others stop believing in me, I push on because

– I can!

Turning to others for help is not easy—however, I do, because

– I can!

Revealing emotions is difficult, but I do because

– I can!

At times, I lack direction and want to give up because

– I can!

But God made me in his image, and whatever I cannot do

He can!

Acknowledgments

I thank the following individuals who inspired me as I journeyed into manhood and assisted me in understanding my worth as a Black male.

Nicholas Vincent, life has thrown you a couple of curve balls, and your willingness to live a productive life is inspirational.

John King Jr., thanks for being a strong and positive Black male. You are inspiration.

Eugenia Davis, thanks for opening up your heart and home.

Gloria Wright, you are one of the realest women I have ever met.

David Greene, thanks for teaching me how to survive and protect my family.

Elisha Gregory, your devotion to family is notable. Thanks for caring.

Danielle Pettis, I love you, little brother. Thanks for having a big heart.

Jeffery Greene, you inspired me as a child. Thanks for being a leader.

Bennie Williams, you believed in me, and I love you for this.

Robert Milton, thanks for showing me how to stand by and support women.

Bettie and Ken Brakebill, thanks for extending loving hearts.

Linda and Bill Sodemann, thanks for not giving up on me.

Stacey Nichols, thanks for being you, and never stop being bighearted.

Keisha Milton, you have been a blessing. Thanks for being a positive woman.

Calvin Nelson, Jr., I appreciate your friendship. Thanks for being you.

Gladys Milton, thanks for accepting me into your heart and family.

Randle Smith, Jr., you inspired me to take that big step— marriage and fatherhood.

William Humphrey, thanks for being a positive friend.

Kevin Bonner, thanks for supporting me over the years.

Jennifer Jones, I truly appreciate your friendship and support. Thanks for offering awesome editorial input.

LaNetra Kellar, I cherish your friendship and thank God for you.

Monica Stephenson, thanks for reintroducing me to Christ. You changed my life.

Bishop Ira Combs, Jr., I will always be grateful for the awesome spiritual guidance.

Thanks to every man and woman that influenced my life and made me who I am today.

Last, but not least, I would like to give a special thanks to my *Pastor John K. Jenkins, Sr.* for his spiritual guidance and wisdom. Thanks for being a superb man of God.

Message to Black Men

You were created in the image of God, and your life was predetermined before you were born. I pray that you look to God for guidance when you are discouraged. I wrote this book with the hope that it will provide tools to help you understand your worth and conquer internalized oppression. As Black men, you experience adversity daily, but your life circumstances do not determine your worth. Your ability to progress in life is determined by your capacity to weather storms with hope and a positive attitude. As a race of people, we have suffered enough. It is time for you to take the lead in restoring our ancestral values and ethics that made the Black community a force to be reckoned with. I pledge to treat each brother with dignity and respect, and I challenge you to do the same. Your efforts will not be in vain. Our women and children are depending on us.

A Message to Black Fathers

I encourage you to take full responsibility for being the head of your household. Life is valued and appreciated by those who understand their position in life. A man who embraces his God-given leadership role will influence those who depend on him. Life's challenges should not deter you from your responsibility to govern yourself like the Conqueror that you are.

"A new dawn of American leadership is at hand."
—President Barack Obama

Black on the Outside, Christian on the Inside

Life as a Christian is easier than Life as an African American

As an African American, I struggle to find peace in this Sinful World, but as a Christian peace finds me.

As an African American, I am judged by my physical attributes, but as a Christian I am judged by the condition of my heart.

As an African American, I am consumed with feelings of bitterness, emptiness and discouragement, but as a Christian I am consumed with feelings of peacefulness, wholeness and hope.

As an African American, I am judged by the steps of my forefathers and mothers, but as a Christian I judged by the steps of my Lord and Savior.

As an African American, I am influenced by Worldly things, but as Christian I am influenced by Godly things.

As an African American, I have the potential to be a great spiritual leader like Dr. Martin Luther King, JR., but as a Christian I have the potential to nurture others and to lead like Jesus Christ.

As an African American, I struggle to connect with and love other ethnic groups, but as Christian connecting with and loving others come with ease.

As an African American, my image is tainted by negative labels such as hostile, aggressive, overbearing, and selfish, but as a Christian my image is illuminated by positive labels such as friendly, considerate, humble, and selfless.

As an African American, my life is influenced by capitalism, racism and violence, but as a Christian my life is influenced by helping the needy, loving thy neighbor and turning the other cheek.

As an African American, I cannot change my skin color nor do I desire to, but as a Christian I can change my attitude and must strive to.

As an African American, I despise diversity because some people use it to justify unruliness, but as Christian I celebrate diversity because it verifies God's creativity.

If I could embrace my role as a Christian as equally as I embrace my role as an African American, my life would be easier.

Diversity should be recognized as a means to celebrate God's creativity, not as a mean to justify unruliness.

- Dr. Dwayne L. Buckingham

Preface

Whilst it is true that race relations and economical opportunities have improved for Blacks over the past few decades, many Black males feel that they are still treated as second class citizens. Traumatized by the historical and on-going effects of oppression, numerous Black males have constructed psychological barriers in order to protect themselves from being re-victimized. This survival and defense mechanism, unfortunately, prevents many of them from leaving communities with limited opportunities; which results in inadequate role models and scarce resources. Feelings of inequality, inadequacy, hopelessness, helplessness, sadness, greed, anger, and hatred are by-products of extreme and prolonged internalized oppression.

Are you suffering from internalized oppression and engaging in self-destructive or self-inhibiting behavior? Internalized oppression is the endorsement of oppressive views and beliefs in negative stereotypes. Individuals experiencing internalized oppression often engage in activities that validate negative stereotypes. For example, many Black males are assumed to be naturally athletic and academically challenged. Individuals who endorse this stereotype will encourage Black males to focus primarily on their athletic gifts instead of academic pursuits. A lot of hours are spent on physical training, but academic preparation is minimal due to an underlying belief that Black males are not smart enough to excel academically. Black males who are suffering from internalized oppression often question their ability to thrive in relationships, in society, and life in general. Internalized oppression might cause you to experience decreased pleasure or satisfaction with self, inability to bond with and trust others, an uncontainable need to please others or to be in control, as well as increased feelings of inferiority, powerlessness, helplessness, and doubtfulness. Internalized oppression may cause you to feel emotionally reserved or restricted and can eventually cause you to self-destruct by engaging in activities that negatively affect you.

Internalized oppression has crippled Black males for decades and continues to be a hindrance to productivity. In an attempt to survive in a capitalistic society, many Black males have adopted the assumptions and methods of their oppressors. A large number of Black males feel inferior, and, in return, treat others as if they are inferior. To minimize their emotional distress, they use money, status, acquired power and/or violence to disempower, marginalize, silence, and control others. This unfortunate reality has prompted countless Black males to suffer from low self-esteem and self-doubt, which is often demonstrated by destroying the Black community and engaging in self-destructive or self-inhibiting behavior.

In pursuit of authority, acceptance, money, power, and respect, some Black males exploit Black women emotionally, physically, and sexually. In addition, some neglect, abuse, and leave their children to cope with life without a father. Like their oppressors, Black males attack, demean, and victimize individuals who are perceived to be inferior. This lack of respect for humanity is justified out of feelings of self-pity and anguish, which are a result of personal and family misfortune. Rationalization takes precedence over common sense and reinforces the vengeful mentality. As Black males, you cannot sit around and blame others for your plight. You must not bombard yourselves with feelings of sympathy and entitlement. You must take the initiative to understand and address this pervasive and destructive trend.

The primary purpose of this book is to serve as a motivational and educational tool for Black males who lack understanding of their worth and therefore struggle to conquer internalized oppression. I greatly appreciate the support and encouragement I have received over the years. I hope to uplift as many Black males as possible. My goal is to help you conquer internalized oppression, which will hopefully help you to understand what it means to be a conqueror and enable you to embrace your responsibility as head of your household.

Contents

Introduction

Am I my brother's keeper? Am I the head of my household? Am I a father to my children? Am I a productive citizen? Am I capable of providing for and protecting my family? Am I capable of coping with adversity in a positive manner?

As a Black male, you were created in the image of God. You are capable of achieving all that your heart desires if you follow God's Will for your life. However, many of you do not live up to your full potential or capitalize on your God-given skills. Why?

Living in an unjust society that continues to oppress Black males has caused many of you to question your right to exist and ability to succeed. Some of you lack direction and struggle to make sense out of your life. In your daily efforts to survive, provide for and protect yourself and others, and feel respected, you fail to understand and embrace God's will for your life. You allow bitterness and disobedience to rob you of what God has already promised you.

God created Adam in his likeness and gave him dominion to care for the earth and to commune with Him directly. He shaped Adam not only to be the head of his household, but to watch over all creation. God's Will for Adam's life was filled with unlimited purpose. Adam was blessed with an opportunity to live in the Garden of Eden eternally, enjoying an everlasting relationship with God. However, Adam failed to embrace what he had been blessed with by disobeying God's commandment to not eat from the tree of knowledge of good and evil. Like Adam, many of you experience hardships because you do not embrace or seek to understand God's Will for your life. So often you complain about not living a prosperous life, but you must remember that God blesses those who are obedient. Adam allowed Eve to persuade him to do wrong despite receiving clear instructions from God. Adam's disobedience and inability to follow God's commands resulted in him being driven out of the Garden of Eden.

The Fall of Man occurred because Adam failed to take control of his household and obey God. God always equips us with instructions to do His Will, but we fail to embrace His guidance. Similar to Adam, your plight is determined by your actions. Hardships you face in life are a direct result of your inability to be a good steward over the things with which you are blessed. God blessed you with the ability to turn despair into hope. Conquering internalized oppression is only possible if you embrace God's Will for your life.

God blessed me to write this book in order to provide you with instructions on how to control your destiny. If you are ready to change your life, you will continue to read this God-inspired book which highlights universal hardships experienced by Black males suffering from internalized oppression. *Seed Thoughts* are presented at the beginning of each chapter in order to stimulate thinking. Each chapter also includes a strategy for males of all ages to help them conquer internalized oppression. R.E.A.L. strategies are provided to help you, but your ability to benefit from them will require you to have an open mind and positive attitude.

To live life without an identity is as harsh as living life without a soul.

——Dwayne L. Buckingham

Does My Life Have Meaning?

----------------------A Black Man's Worth!----------------------

---------- *Chapter 1* ----------

For centuries, man has sought answers to two fundamental questions regarding human existence: Does my life have meaning? and Who am I? Defining and giving meaning to one's life is very important. Most men live their lives trying to accomplish this goal. Knowledge of self and why we exist provides a road map for living our lives and helps shape our souls. *To live life without an identity is as harsh as living life without a soul.* I believe that every man's life is significant, but how does one determine if his life is meaningful? In modern day society, most people believe that their lives are meaningful if they possess power, wealth, fame, money, and wisdom. Most expect to be protected from violence, receive suitable education, be supported emotionally, mentored or guided when faced with life challenges, and to be granted equal employment opportunities.

As a Black male growing up in urban America, I thought that my life and the lives of other Black males were insignificant and dispensable. Why? To help you better understand those feelings, I would like you to join me as I reminisce. We will take a look at personal hardships and challenges I experienced as a Black male living in this rigid and unjust society. Are you ready?

As a child I was often told that I could be whatever I wanted to be. Despite my speech impediment, I was a normal and healthy child whose life was filled with promise and hope. I was destined for greatness. I never questioned my ability to succeed or maintain a positive sense of self. Like many hopeful Black males living in urban America, I believed that my skin color, developmental delay, nor environmental conditions would be crippling factors in my effort to achieve the "American" dream. I was optimistic and saw the world through the eyes of those who nurtured, sheltered, and shielded me.

I anticipated starting school with excitement and eagerness. I was told that school would help me develop skills that would enable me to conquer the world. However, as I left my sheltered home environment, I was exposed to the reality of living in a harsh and unjust society. My neighborhood was shabby, and the streets were filled with men who sought power, money, and control through the use of violence, drugs, and crime. The school I attended was like a war zone where violence occurred daily. To make matters worse, I was teased daily at school by my peers for having a speech impediment. I did not know how to cope with the teasing, so I shut down and refused to express myself. As a result, my teachers quickly labeled me as being "defiant" and as a "behavioral problem". They tried to force me to participate in class, but I resisted. I was willing to accept the consequences as long as it prevented me from being teased. No one every asked me why I refused to follow their instructions; instead I was punished. The place that previously filled me with excitement had become my nightmare. I resorted to fighting to stop my peers from teasing me. Dishing out and receiving punishment was a vicious cycle in my life. I thrashed my peers, my teachers thrashed me, and then my mother and older siblings thrashed me again when I arrived home. With this drama in my life, I definitely was not focused on excelling in school. In fact, I ended up repeating the second grade. Now in the same grade as my younger brother, my self-esteem was low and my ego was crushed. My view of myself and life began to change.

As I continued to explore my environment, I witnessed violence, murder, and police brutality and harassment daily. It was not long before my hopes turned to despair. At age seven, I began to ask myself *Does my life have meaning?* I grew up viewing myself and other Black males negatively. I thought all Black men were sadistic because they did horrible things that were destructive to themselves and others.

While riding down the street with my mother and older brother, my mother's ex-boyfriend shot at the car, and I was hit in the arm. He was angry because my mother ended their relationship. At this point in my life, I was already miserable and numb to emotional pain, so the shooting did not significantly affect me. *I believed wholeheartedly that my life was dispensable. I hoped for the best, but expected the worst.*

Life was filled with disappointment. The man who was supposed to be my father told me that he was not because I made him angry. With all the madness and destruction around me, I found peace in learning how to dissociate from my surroundings to feel safe. I dreamed about being a doctor who healed the sick. I did whatever I could to maintain a positive view of myself as a Black male. However, this coping mechanism slowly faded as I was reminded daily of my reality. There were no doctors walking the streets of my neighborhood. I could not identify with the lifestyle of a doctor. However, I was very familiar with the lifestyle of drug dealers, gangsters, and blue collar workers. I was confused and did not understand why my lifestyle did not resemble the lifestyle of white children I watched on television. They were protected from violence, received suitable education, were supported emotionally, mentored when faced with life challenges, and their parents were granted equal and viable employment opportunities. My mind drifted regularly. It was difficult for me to distinguish between fantasy and reality.

I often fantasized about living in a community where I could walk out my door and not worry about being shot, offered drugs, or jumped by bullies. I fantasized about living where I could receive suitable education. I fantasized about having positive male role models who could help me cope with life challenges. I fantasized about having a father present who could help my mother take care of us and relieve her financial burden. As my fantasies grew, so did my awareness of my reality. I lived in a one-bedroom apartment in the ghetto with my mother, younger brother, and sister. I fought to survive and protect myself from bullies. I attended schools that were substandard and was educated by teachers who were underpaid and burnt-out. I looked to my peers to help me cope with life challenges because I did not have positive adult male role models. My teen years were difficult for me. I struggled with my reality. Again, I began to question my existence. *Does my life have meaning?*

I was bitter as a teenager and engaged in behaviors that were familiar to me. I exploited young girls sexually for self-gratification and used violence against those who threatened my "manhood" or ability to survive. I did not care about my life and had little concern for others. At times I even struggled to love family members and friends who did not express love for me, at least not in a way that I could appreciate. As I experienced personal hardships, my bitterness grew, and I eventually turned to the streets for understanding and acceptance. My peers were struggling with similar hardships and understood my misery. They also questioned their existence and desperately sought to understand meaning in their lives. We found comfort in each other's despair. We wanted nice things and security, but most importantly, we wanted to be loved, understood, and accepted. We developed a brotherhood built on pain, misery, and anguish. Life in the "hood" was intolerable at times, so we promised to support each other financially, physically, and emotionally. We observed others, studied our environment, and learned to identity weak individuals. We targeted young girls who displayed an inferiority complex, and brothers who could not "bang".

As you are reading this, you are probably thinking that our behavior was wrong and cruel. Yes! I agree now, but then I did not see anything wrong with my behavior. After all, I did not care about my own life. The behavior I engaged in was commonly practiced. I did not feel guilty. Experiencing and inflicting pain was normal. How could I find it within myself to love, respect, and treat others justly when my life was filled with fear, disappointment, and pain? I was a hurt young boy trying to find *"meaning"* in my life.

In existentialism, *"meaning"* is understood as the worth of life. Existentialism is a philosophical movement which posits that individuals create the meaning and essence of their lives, as opposed to it being created for them by God or theological doctrines. Although I was a Christian and believed in God, I felt that I could create *meaning* for my life. I did not understand why I was born into poverty and was not privileged to possess power, wealth, fame, or money. I was not protected from violence and did not receive suitable education, emotional support, or mentoring when I was faced with life challenges. Employment opportunities were scarce in my community, but crime was pervasive. I felt cursed. I was a hurt, fatherless child trying to find *meaning* in my life. My mother encouraged me to pray and turn to God for peace. I believed my mother and did exactly as I was told. However, after years of praying, my life and environment did not change. I continued to believe in God, but decided to answer my own prayers and create my own *meaning* for my life.

I turned to the streets. Some say that hustling does not pay, but in my neighborhood, it appeared to be the only thing that paid. Hustlers were respected and admired. They had nice cars, women and all the finer things in life. They provided for their families and eventually moved out of the ghetto. Hustlers had it all. They did not go to school or pray to God. Everybody knew the big time hustlers. It was cool to have money. I learned that money made the world go around. Those who possessed it were in positions to define their own life as well as other's lives. Survival of the fittest was a commonly held belief. Many hustlers obtained their power and wealth by exploiting individuals who were in pain or looking for an opportunity to improve their status. To be a successful hustler, you had to learn to suppress your emotions in order to prevent the lifestyle from destroying you.

At age fourteen, I began to live the lucrative lifestyle of a hustler. I was introduced to the lifestyle by one of my peers. He was fourteen years old as well, but had begun his career as a hustler at age thirteen. I often questioned him about the expensive jewelry and clothes he wore. I knew that he was not old enough to work, and his mother was not wealthy, as she was a single parent struggling to make ends meet just like my mother. One day he took me into his house and educated me about hustling. He explained that hustling was easy and informed me that I could earn money quickly. However, he did not explain that hustling was illegal and that I could be arrested. Naïve and excited, I quickly exited his house and ran to the streets. Within twenty minutes, I had accumulated one hundred and twenty-five dollars. This newfound wealth made me feel good about myself. I could purchase some of the things my heart desired. I found happiness in money and felt important.

I lived this lifestyle in secrecy for several years while attending school regularly, playing sports, and maintaining average grades. I took advantage of the fact that my mother worked long hours. She was an easygoing woman who did not feel the need to question my whereabouts or daily activities as long as I stayed out of trouble. I wanted to tell her about my life as a hustler, but I knew she would knock my head off. She was old school and believed in working hard and living righteously. She consistently attempted to instill the fear of God in my siblings and me. Going to church was not an option. My mother was a loving woman who exemplified qualities that I liked and did not like. She was strong, spiritual, and hardworking, but we were poor. We lived with other family members from time to time and survived the best we could. My mother did everything she could to make life good for my siblings and me, but often felt bad because she could not give us what our hearts desired. It hurt me to see my mother in distress. I used my family's predicament to justify living a life of transgression. I enjoyed the fruits of my labor as a hustler, but my conscious and personal hardships would eventually drive me to quit. On a day-to-day basis, I witnessed the senseless destruction of my community. My friends' mothers were addicted to crack and would sell their bodies to teenage boys for hits. I watched pregnant women use crack with no concern for the life inside of them. I also watched fighting over drug turf and money as gangs dominated the community. Neighborhoods were divided by Cripps or Blood affiliation. Individuals were beaten or murdered every day for wearing the wrong colors in the wrong hood. The destruction began to affect me mentally. I was not raised to hurt or take advantage of others. I was an emotional wreck still seeking to understand the *meaning* of my life. In the mist of my emotional chaos and confusion, I lost the only woman I truly loved. My mother passed after my junior year in high school, after suffering from brain cancer for a few months.

Prior to my mother's death, I could not truly relate to my peers' anguish and pain about being parentless. However, after I lost my mother, my anguish intensified. I did not understand why God took my mother from me while I was so young. I had already been deprived by growing up without a father, and now I had to live without my mother, the only person who loved me unconditionally. My mother's death caused me to question my existence again. *Does my life have meaning?*

I found no pleasure in continuing to hurt others, especially after I experienced pain first-hand. I knew that I wanted to do something with my life. I was fortunate enough to attend a predominantly white high school where ninety percent of graduates attended college. I met with my guidance counselor frequently, and she took me under her wing. She provided what I longed for. I wanted to be accepted by someone outside of the Black community. I longed for guidance, and she represented what I saw on television. She lived in a safe environment and possessed knowledge that I believed could help me turn my fantasies into reality. With the assistance of my counselor, basketball coach, and other school officials, I applied and secured admission to Jackson State University in Mississippi. I was excited as I realized that this was my opportunity to escape my misery, but my excitement was short lived. I did not have money to attend college. My anguish resurfaced as I was reminded of my reality—I was poor. I applied for financial aid, but missed the deadline.

With my back against the wall, I decided to revisit a lifestyle I was very familiar with. *I was willing to lose my freedom in order to be freed.* I promised God that I would never hustle again if He allowed me to earn enough money to enroll in college. I hit the block and within one month, I acquired sufficient funds. Life was finally looking up for me. Inspired for the first time in a long time, I was headed to Jackson State University.

I was the first out of eight children to be accepted into college, and I could not wait to start my new life. Filled with pride, I left for Mississippi at 12:00 a.m. This was my first road trip, and my inexperience as a highway driver almost cost me my life. After driving six and one-half hours, I fell asleep at the steering wheel, ran into a ditch, and hit a tree. My car was totaled, but I walked away with only a cut on my nose. I thanked God for my life, but my spirit was crushed once again. I eventually made it to campus, but spent the first few days in my dorm room. I was depressed. I sat on my bed wondering if my curse would ever be lifted. Again, I asked myself *Does my life have meaning?*

My obsession with understanding the meaning of my life consumed me. A day did not go by that I was not trying to figure out the significance of my life and understand why I continued to experience hardships. As I selected classes to begin my college career, I carefully read each curriculum and enrolled in classes that addressed human behavior and development. I was finally in an environment that provided some security and opportunities to learn. I took my education very seriously. I applied myself one hundred percent and accumulated a 4.0 grade point average my first semester. I was proud, but not surprised. I knew I had what it took to make it in life, but I lacked guidance, encouragement, and wisdom.

College was an environment that was filled with progressive Black males who were striving to make their lives better by acquiring knowledge that would empower them. After engaging in several stimulating conversations about disadvantaged populations with my counselor, I decided to major in social work. College was a safe haven for me, and I was stimulated intellectually. However, I continued to suffer emotionally.

At age nineteen, I received a phone call informing me that my eighteen-year-old nephew was convicted of murder and sentenced to double life in prison without parole. The news was devastating, so I decided to return to St. Louis for a short vacation and to comfort my sister. While on vacation, I was robbed at gun point in broad daylight after visiting the library in downtown. The perpetrator was arrested and sentenced to five years due to my testimony. As I entered my sophomore year, the drama did not stop. At age twenty, I received another phone call informing me that my best friend from childhood was arrested and sentenced to five years in prison for drug charges. At age twenty-one, I attended my seventeen-year-old nephew's funeral after he was gunned down while walking home from the store. No arrest was made. At age twenty-two, I received a phone call informing me that one of my close friends was murdered due to an attempted robbery gone bad. At age twenty-three, I attended my thirty-four-year-old cousin's funeral; my nephew accidentally shot him while playing with a gun. At age twenty-four, I received a phone call informing me that my close friend was shot during an attempted robbery.

The violence and death was disheartening, but I was determined to succeed. I excelled in college and successfully graduated with honors. A year later, I secured a master's degree in social work from Michigan State University. After graduate school, I joined the military and lived a comfortable lifestyle as a Captain in the United States Air Force. Life was good, as I had acquired material items I longed for and was in a position of authority. I felt good about my accomplishments, but I was still not happy. I felt empty. I moved frequently in search of something to fill my void. I was an emotional wreck seeking to understand the *meaning* of my life and, over time, became very bitter.

As my bitterness grew, I decided to reflect on childhood teachings from my mother. My mother often spoke of a God who could provide all that my heart desired. She encouraged me to pray and reassured me that God would not forsake me. As I thought about the teachings I received from my mother, I realized that I was searching to find *meaning* for my life in all the wrong places. The answer to my question could not be found in psychology or philosophy books; people or material things. My mother, like our ancestors, believed that God could heal wounded hearts and repair damaged souls. *She preached that any man who lived a life without God, lived a meaningless life.* I thanked God for giving me the gift of reflection and showed my gratitude by restoring my relationship with Him.

Through fellowship with other Christians and studying the *Word*, I learned that my life is *meaningful* because I am a *Child of God*, and He created me so that one day I can inherit His kingdom. Luke 12:32, "Fear not, little flock; for it is your Father's good pleasure to give you the kingdom."

To further understand the *meaning* of my life, I began to study the Bible daily and attended church and Bible study weekly. As I studied the *Word*, I also learned that my sole purpose in life was to serve God. The scripture says, "Serve the Lord with gladness; Come before His presence with singing. Know that the Lord, He is God; It is He who has made us, and not we ourselves; We are His people and the sheep of His pasture" (Psalms 100:2-3). My Christian experience taught me that God created me to serve Him on the basis of love. God's *Word* instructs us to trust in Him with all our hearts and do not lean on our own understanding. In all our ways, acknowledge Him, and He will make our paths straight (Proverbs 3:5-6). As a result of my spiritual growth and basic understanding of the *Word*, I learned that life does not have *meaning* without God's presence, and that if He is for me, no man can be against me. Therefore, we must turn to God in our time of distress, and he will save us, "Then they cry unto the Lord in their trouble, he saveth them out of their distresses." (Psalms 107:19). However, if we desire to have a relationship with God and serve Him, we must free ourselves from sin in order to be made holy, blameless, and sanctified. Serving God is the only way we will find *meaning* in our lives. He did not create us to worship ourselves, things, or others. My void was not filled, and I did not understand the *meaning* for my life until I turned to God.

As a result of restoring my relationship with God, I acquired knowledge that helped me understand the *meaning* of my life. I spent many years believing and feeling that I was fatherless, but He was with me always. I did not have a nice home, but I was not homeless. I did not have hot water, but I bathed. I did not have nice clothes, but I was clothed. I did not eat expensive food, but I was not hungry. I was shot in the arm, but not killed. I was robbed at gun point, but not killed. I fell asleep while driving my car to college, but not killed. I was hit by a drunken driver and my car was demolished, but I was not killed. I witnessed and faced death, but I was spared. I did not receive suitable education as a child, but now I have two college degrees. I did not come from a wealthy family, but now I visit other countries yearly, and all my needs are met. I did not receive mentoring or emotional support, but now I am a clinical social worker who provides both.

Please take a moment and reflect on what you just read. I want you to understand how great God is. He was preparing me to be a conqueror and head of my household, and I am honored to be His disciple. As His disciple, I understand that my short stay in this world filled with pain and sorrow is temporary. So often we dwell in such misery that we cannot see the goodness in our lives. I thank God for His infinite goodness, and I pray that you look to Him to find *meaning* for your life as I did. The reward will be eternal. He never abandoned me, and He hasn't abandoned you.

18

Questions for Reflection and Discussion

Does your life have meaning?
Yes____ No_____ (Explain)

Can you give meaning to your life?
Yes____ No_____ (Explain)

Can your life be meaningful without God?
Yes____ No_____ (Explain)

Where can you turn to find meaning in your life?

What is the purpose of your life?

Does God ever forsake us?
Yes____ No_____ (Explain)

Use the space below to record your feelings and/or thoughts about this chapter. What did you learn?

*Notes*_____

_____
_____
_____
_____
_____
_____
_____
_____
_____
_____
_____
_____
_____
_____
_____
_____
_____
_____
_____
_____
_____
_____
_____
_____
_____

I have learned that success is to be measured not so much by the position that one has reached in life, as by the obstacles which he has overcome while trying to succeed.

—Booker T. Washington

Conqueror and Head of Household

---------- *Chapter 2* ----------

It is imperative to comprehend what it means to be a conqueror and head of your household. Your ability to weather storms is greatly influenced by your comprehension of this concept. A conqueror is a person who is persistent. He does not operate out of fear or quit when faced with adversity. A conqueror looks at adversity as a lesson and presses on until he accomplishes his desire outcome. Before I further enlighten you, I would like to make it clear that being a conqueror does not mean that you will not suffer. Jesus suffered tremendously as a conqueror. His persecution was not just in words, but in physical beatings (Matthews 26:67-68; 27; 26-31), and He was taunted even as He was being killed (Mark 15:29-32). Let's be clear, any man that walks this sinful earth is subject to harm. God gave all men the gift of Free Will. Some choose to use the gift for evil. If you truly believe that God is good, why do you believe that He allows bad things to happen? Blaming God for man's wrongdoing demonstrates a lack of understanding regarding the true essence of His nature. God is good all the time, and all the time, God is good. With that said, the first thing you must do to learn what it means to be a conqueror is study the *Word*. If you live by His Word, He will protect you. Every Word of God is flawless; He is a shield to those who take refuge in him (Proverbs 30:5)

   Secondly, as a conqueror, you are required to surrender your life to God. Occasionally, we like to take matters into our own hands and rely on our own means. But God demands that we surrender to His will in all our endeavors. We must learn to walk in faith and know that God will provide as promised. We must also remember that the battle is His and not ours. Being submissive pleases God and demonstrates faith. We were created to submit to and obey Him, and only Him. However, because we are human, we will occasionally test our Father. Our disobedient nature causes suffering, but He is a merciful God who realizes that disobedience helps us grow as well. For this reason, He continues to provide opportunities for us to live righteously. He is faithful to those who are faithful to Him, and He will fight and win the battle for you.

Third, as a conqueror you must learn to forgive others for their unruliness. God will deal with those who hurt, belittle, humiliate, disgrace, or oppress you. Taking matters into your own hands displays a lack of confidence in God. He will judge and persecute all wrong doers. A heart of forgiveness is required of all God's children. Forgiveness is the only way you will be able to remove despair, bitterness, and hatred from your heart. Jesus suffered at the hands of evil men and did not retaliate. He allowed his offenders to be judged by the One who judges fairly (1 Peter 2:23).

Finally, as a conqueror you are commanded to love God with all your heart and love thy neighbor as thyself. What does this mean? God does not need our love to feel whole; He is already complete. Therefore, He expects us to demonstrate our love for Him by loving and serving our brethren. Selfishness has no place in God's kingdom. Life is preserved by His grace and compassion, and He commands us to show compassion for others. All of God's children desire to have a home, food, and clothes. Each one of us is responsible for comforting our brethren in distress, feeding brethren who are hungry, clothing brethren who do not have clothes, housing brethren who are homeless, and speaking kind words to brethren who are mean or cruel to us. Being a conqueror is not an easy task. Non believers will curse and scorn you. Are you prepared to be persecuted? Will you rejoice in your persecution? To live righteously in this sinful world is not easy, but setting the example for others is important.

As head of your household, you set the tempo. "You reap what you sow" (Galatians 6:7). The seeds you plant (sow) will lead to your resulting harvest (reap). The quality of your harvest depends on the kind of seeds you sow. If you sow chaos, you will not reap harmony. If you expect others to do as you wish, exemplify the desired behavior. The adage "Do as I say, not as I do" is old and irrational. If you desire respect, demonstrate it. If you desire to have others submit to you, be willing to submit yourself. If you desire others to show personal integrity, live righteously, admit your wrongs, and strive to overcome them.

It is your responsibility to demonstrate personal integrity, foster love and independence, provide guidance, and be accountable for your actions (1 Corinthians 11:3; Ephesians 5:23). However, you were not given authority to lead in a dictatorial, arrogant, or belittling manner. You are commanded to treat your wife in accordance with how Christ led the Church. Show her compassion, mercy, forgiveness, respect and demonstrate your love through selflessness. And in regards to your children, Proverbs 22:6 makes it clear that it is your responsibility to train them in the way they should go, and when they are older, they should not depart from your teachings. Set the example by living it.

If you are to conquer internalized oppression, it must begin at home. Do not expect members of society to stop oppressing you if you are not willing to stop oppressing your family members and others. If you are not married, but date, I encourage you to approach and treat women in the same manner you would expect another man to treat your mother, sister, or daughter. What goes around comes around. Love and admiration should drive your relationships; not control, disrespect, and disempowerment.

Understanding and embracing your role as a conqueror and head of your household will enable you to build a solid family that will stand firm when adversity comes. Similarly, encourage the young men in your household to be self-controlled. In everything set them an example by doing what is good. In your teaching show integrity, seriousness and soundness of speech that cannot be condemned, so that those who oppose you may be ashamed because they have nothing bad to say about you (Titus 2: 7-8).

Questions for Reflection and Discussion

Do you know what it means to be a conqueror and head of your household?

If God is good, why do you believe He allows bad things to happen?

What does it mean to love God with all thy heart?

What does it mean to surrender to God?

Why is it important to forgive others? (Explain)

Use the space below to record your feelings and/or thoughts about this chapter. What did you learn?

*Notes*_____

_____
_____
_____
_____
_____
_____
_____
_____
_____
_____
_____
_____
_____
_____
_____
_____
_____
_____
_____
_____
_____
_____
_____
_____
_____
_____
_____
_____
_____
_____
_____

"And as we let our light shine, we unconsciously give other people permission to do the same. As we're liberated from our own fear, our presence automatically liberates others."

—*Nelson Mandela*

A R.E.A.L. Man

---------- *Chapter 3* ----------

What makes a man a *REAL* man? I am glad you asked. Perceptions regarding what a *REAL* man is, or is not, vary and are subjective. As young Black males enter manhood, many struggle with developing positive and healthy self-concepts. Let's review some commonly held perceptions about what a *REAL* man is and explore how they can cause or contribute to self-inhibiting or self-destructive behavior.

- A *REAL* man is strong and does not cry or show sensitive emotions!
- A *REAL* man is self-sufficient and does not need help!
- A *REAL* man is brave and does not back down!
- A *REAL* man is proud and does not apologize!

"A REAL man is strong and does not cry or show sensitive emotions" is often expressed to remind males to maintain their manhood. "Do not act feminine." Expressing sensitive or nurturing emotions, or giving freely, is not praised or encouraged. The pressure to maintain masculinity and remain strong often creates emotional roadblocks. For example, if a little boy falls down and begins to cry, he is told that "big boys do not cry". In harsher words, he might be told to "stop crying you little punk; crying is for girls". *Little boys who do not cry become men who do not cry.*

Feelings of remorse, forgiveness, sadness, and empathy are overshadowed by feelings of self-pity, anger, embarrassment, pride, and hatred. Many of you have a desire to express sensitive emotions and demonstrate compassion, but lack the capacity because you were not taught properly. Your perceptions of manhood are built on false beliefs. You minimize or suppress sensitive emotions in order to appear to maintain your masculinity. Often you become defensive or feel frustrated and angry when someone questions your masculinity. Your increased emotional distress often leads to a refusal to express sadness or pain in a sensitive or appropriate manner.

Words of affection are viewed as a sign of weakness and are expressed only in desperate situations, i.e. the end of a relationship, pending divorce, separation from or death of loved ones, etc. This self-inhibiting behavior contributes to the conflict experienced in many of your relationships. Instead of saying "I am sorry" or "I was wrong", many of you will allow your relationships to end, leave your children, jobs, and even resort to violence. Bottled-up negative emotions are a recipe for disaster. Crying and the expression of other sensitive emotions releases stress and shows profound love and concern for others.

Brothers, I challenge you to stop worrying about what others will think about you and learn to express affection for others. Expression of sensitive emotions does not convey that you are weak or feminine; it does convey that you are compassionate. God created humans, both men and women, with a full range of emotions because He understood that we could not appreciate happiness without sadness, calmness without anger, laughter without crying, innocence without guilt, and love without hate. Expressing sensitive emotions is natural and does not inhibit you from experiencing and sharing what's in your heart. A R.E.A.L. man does not limit his ability to express the God-given emotions he was blessed with. *Behind every action there is an emotion.* Learn to acknowledge and express sensitive emotions and hopefully you will receive sensitive responses. The "tough man, I don't care" attitude only distances others from you. You get what you give. Do not let this homophobic society prevent you from sharing your gift of compassion. It is okay to show affection toward another man. An individual needs a good balance of all expressions of emotion to be most healthy.

"A REAL man is self-sufficient and does not need help" is used to encourage males to feel that they can make it through life single-handily or with little help. I agree that it is important to be self-sufficient. If people are satisfied with their needs, they will be less greedy. With less greed, they will cause less trouble to other people. People who are sufficient are usually *proud* of their accomplishments. However, they also struggle to ask for help when needed. Why? – Too much pride. At some point in our lives, we all will require assistance from others, but some men are too proud to ask for help. This self-inhibiting behavior often increases suffering. As your distress increases and your pride intensifies, it becomes more difficult to ask for help, and the destructive process begins. In His infinite wisdom, God created Eve because he knew man needed a helpmate. I pray that you do not let your pride prevent you from reaching out to others.

"A REAL man is brave and does not back down" is used to encourage males to stand firm. I have seen several Black males use this approach, and unfortunately, have lost their lives, jobs, and relationships. Many men confuse bravery with ignorance. Bravery is the ability to confront fear, pain, risk/danger, uncertainty, or intimidation. And ignorance is the condition of knowing something but refusing to take notice of it. If you realize that something is dangerous or unhealthy for you, and you chose to pursue it, you might be operating out of ignorance. For example, if you are attacked by several individuals, and you fight back, you might be considered brave. However, if you attack or chose to fight several individuals, you might be considered ignorant. Losing your life or being hurt severely is not manly. You only have one life, and if you live it correctly, you will have many opportunities to demonstrate your bravery.

"A REAL man is proud and does not apologize". I agree that every man should be proud; however, no man is too important to apologize or give compliments to others, especially if they are deserving of them. The Bible says that pride leads to disgrace (Proverbs 11:2); produces quarrels (Proverbs 13:10); leads to punishment (Proverbs 16:5); and destruction (Proverbs 16:18). Too much pride and love for yourself will distance you from God. Once you learn humility, then giving compliments and apologizing to others will come easy.

In my opinion, the "REAL" man perception has created emotional distress and confusion for many Black males. I have personally witnessed some of you engaging in destructive and self-inhibiting behavior in an attempt to sustain this "REAL" man facade. For example, having sex with multiple women to demonstrate that you are a REAL man; emotionally and physically abusing your women and children because you believe that a REAL man is capable of controlling others; and refusing to leave communities with limited resources and positive role models because a REAL man does not sell out. This persistent devotion to prove your manhood, especially to other Black males, can prove to be destructive to your emotional and physical health as well as others.

Many of you have an intense need to feel respected and empowered. Some will resort to aggressive means if you feel disrespected or disempowered. I have heard some Black males say they would engage in destructive or violent behavior such as beating or shooting another individual to secure respect: "I don't care what I have to do, but I will not be disrespected. I am a REAL man and no one is going to test my manhood." I have also heard brothers say they are willing to walk away from relationships if they feel threatened. "I don't like to be questioned or made to feel like I am not needed. If a woman cannot stroke my ego, then I don't need her. A REAL man does not deal with women who are not submissive." How many of you have found yourself saying this? Why do you engage in and facilitate such behavior? What does being a REAL man mean to you? Will you hurt yourself and/or others to sustain this REAL man façade? Believe me, I understand your pain and need to be in control, but I challenge you to think about the impending harsh consequences of living by the REAL man perception. Why are you so concerned about impressing others? Why do you continue to engage in destructive or self-inhibiting behavior if you know right from wrong? Is being a REAL man that important?

Can I offer a little advice? A REAL man does not self-destruct or harm others. A REAL man strives to improve his life and the lives of others in a healthy and productive manner. A "R.E.AL." man lives his life as a conqueror and head of his household. To help you understand my perception of what a "R.E.A.L." man is, I formulated an uplifting and heartfelt concept. Throughout the following chapters, REAL is spelled "R.E.A.L." It is written in this manner to help you grasp the concept below.

A **R**.E.A.L. man approaches situations in a *Realistic* manner. He expresses an awareness of things as they are, but uses sound judgment and demonstrates empathy for others. He also seeks to understand the source of his problems and others before he attempts to address them.

A R.**E**.A.L. man exercises sound reasoning in order to develop rational *Expectations* or beliefs. He realizes that the expectations he has about himself, others, and life in general will reflect how he lives his life. He strives to eliminate irrational expectations and replaces them with rational ones.

A R.E.**A**.L. man maintains a positive *Attitude* and image of himself and others. He does not allow his attitude or feelings to prevent him from being happy or progressing in life. He understands that negativity begets negativity, and he controls his destiny.

A R.E.A.**L**. man develops unconditional *Love* for himself and others. He establishes a deep, tender, indefinable feeling of affection and attentiveness toward himself and others that is not determined or influenced by someone or something.

In summary, a "*R.E.A.L.*" man strives to expand his horizons (cognitive, behavioral, and social skills) by approaching situations realistically, with rational expectations, a positive attitude, and unconditional love. A R.E.A.L man realizes that his purpose in life is to live according to God's Will and not his own. God created you to have a relationship with Him. I do not intend to offend or judge you, but I am simply asking you to examine your lifestyle and determine if you are living it like a "R.E.A.L." man. What impact do you have on the people you interact with? Are you uplifting or negative? Do you live a servant lifestyle? Jesus was not concerned with ruling or controlling people, nor was He concerned with what others did to him. Live to let go and learn to serve others. This posture of servitude will enable you to grow in ways you could not imagine. If you are not conducting yourself like a "R.E.A.L." man, I challenge you to continue reading and I promise that the remaining chapters will provide the guidance you need to live as a conqueror and head of your household, which will optimistically help you become a "R.E.A.L" man who is capable of conquering internalized oppression.

--------------------A R.E.A.L. Man--------------------

Questions for Reflection and Discussion

What makes a man a REAL man?

What are some common misperceptions about a REAL man?

What does it mean to be a REAL man to you?

Will you self-destruct or harm others to prove you are a REAL man?

What does it mean to be a R.E.A.L. man? (Explain)

Use the space below to record your feelings and/or thoughts about this chapter. What did you learn?

*Notes*_____

_____

_____

_____

_____

_____

_____

_____

_____

_____

_____

_____

_____

_____

_____

_____

_____

_____

_____

_____

_____

_____

_____

_____

_____

_____

_____

_____

_____

_____

_____

In America, anyone can still become somebody.

—*Jesse Owens*

Be Realistic

---------- *Chapter 4* ----------

Like me, many Black males go through life with significant hate, despair, pain, and sorrow in their hearts. Hopelessness and helplessness is common and often exhibited through destructive interactions with loved ones, friends, co-workers, and people in general. With a lack of guidance and access to mental health professionals in the Black community, many Black males do not receive the support they need to understand and cope with unhealthy emotions. Some realize that they are not emotionally stable, but suppress their emotions because they lack insight into their emotions or the ability to cope with them. This temporary coping mechanism works until excessive distress becomes unbearable, causing feelings of anger, hate, despair, hopelessness, helplessness, and bitterness to resurface. During this negative emotional cycle, you lash out physically and emotionally against those who are close to you. And after years of broken relationships, job dissatisfaction, personal and interpersonal problems, and continued hardships, you decide to distance yourself from others. You desire to maintain relationships, but never give totally of yourself. Additionally, you indulge yourself with trivial material items to feel good. Life appears to be good at times, however, you continue to fail to address your underlying emotional issues. Like a merry-go-round, you spin and spin, but never change direction.

The process of losing weight is similar to that of understanding oppression. There are several steps you must take to prepare yourself to lose weight. First, and most important, is the ability to develop a new eating and exercise routine that will allow you to keep the weight off. If you fail to establish and maintain a new regimen, the weight will come back quickly, and you will eventually become discouraged. Therefore, to keep the weight off permanently, you must understand what is required to maintain your desired outcome. A *"R.E.A.L."* man realizes that he cannot correct a problem unless he understands the underlying cause and equips himself to deal with it.

Understanding Oppression

Realizing what oppression is, and how it affected you, is the first strategy to conquering internalized oppression. According to the Wikipedia, oppression is the act of using power to empower and/or privilege a group at the expense of disempowering, marginalizing, silencing, and subordinating another. Oppression is sustained by individuals who believe that a certain group of people are inferior. Learning about oppression significantly enhanced my understanding of why so many Black males are consumed by feelings of anger, hate, despair, hopelessness, helplessness, and bitterness.

Greater understanding increases one's ability to cope with or tolerate hardships. And for this reason, your ability to conquer internalized oppression begins and ends with your understanding. *A man who cannot control his emotions positions himself to be controlled by others.* Undeniably, you are God's most **resilient** creation. However, your inability and/or unwillingness to understand and conquer oppression also make you God's most **destructive** creation.

Over and over again, you neglect to schedule time to address emotions that negatively affect you. This unhealthy coping mechanism has caused long drawn-out suffering. In order to conquer internalized oppression and live a life with minimum distress, you must first understand how it evolved. Some believe that history repeats itself. What do you think?

Learn your History

Throughout history, Black males have been oppressed and have, in return, internalized this oppression. To help you grasp the impact oppression has had on Black males, I would like you to join me on a voyage down heritage lane. While on our journey, we will review decades of hardships experienced by Black males:

- **Slavery;**
- **Jim Crow Era; and**
- **Civil Rights Era.**

Black males who experience extreme trauma and suffering are at greater risk for internalizing their experience. Maintain an open mind as we journey down heritage lane to review qualities that some Black males acquired from those who oppressed them. Below are a few quotations that are intended to stimulate thinking as we begin our voyage.

Men rise from one ambition to another – first they seek to secure themselves from attack, and then they attack others.
—Machiavelli

Man, biologically considered...is the most formidable of all the beasts of prey, and indeed the only one that preys systematically on his own species.
—William James

Injustice anywhere is a threat to justice everywhere.
—Dr. Martin Luther King

Those who make peaceful change impossible will make violent revolution inevitable.

—John F. Kennedy

Traveling on this voyage will greatly enhance your understanding of why you and other Black males struggle to cope with negative emotions. As we explore our past, you may experience an array of negative emotions: sadness and anger; hate and bitterness; but at the end of our voyage, I promise you will be informed. Buckle down and prepare yourself for the adventure that will revolutionize your view of yourself forever. Are you ready? Let's go. We'll start our voyage by reviewing the institution of slavery.

Source: Wikipedia

Slavery was a social-economic structure under which slaves were deprived of personal freedom and forced to work. Slavery began in the early 1600's after the English colonists first settled in Virginia, and lasted until the Thirteenth Amendment to the U.S. Constitution. Slaves were held against their will from the time of their capture, purchase, or birth, and were deprived of the right to leave, to refuse to work, or to receive compensation in return for their labor. As such, slavery was one form of free labor. Basically, the

--------------------Be Realistic--------------------

word slave referred to citizens who were treated as the property of another person, household, company, corporation, or government. This was referred to as chattel slavery. Slavery was a formal system designed to subordinate a certain group by unjust use of force, authority, or societal norms, and was legal within the boundaries of United States. Most slaves were Black and engaged in an efficient machine-like gang system of agriculture. Most slaves were held by planters who achieved wealth and social and political power. Slaves were considered non-legal persons or things that were incapable of performing civil acts, and to maintain control and order, slave owners beat, separated, and even murdered slaves who rebelled. *Sexual exploitation and abuse of Black women was rampant and occurred in front of Black males.* Slavery was an institution that traumatized Black males both mentally and physically. No one can truly determine the psychological damage that slavery caused, but most people agree that Black males were significantly affected. Men who were once referred to as Kings and Warriors were powerless. They could not protect their women or children and were forced to witness their destruction. Slavery drastically influenced how Black males viewed themselves and life in general. Many suppressed feelings of helplessness, hopelessness, despair, sadness, and anger to survive and cope with their harsh conditions. They were expected to work hard and keep their feelings inside. They were taught to be strong and never show weakness. *They were taught to survive, not live,* and destruction and violence was imposed on those who did not comply. Undoubtedly, slavery laid the foundation for the self-destructive and self-inhibiting behavior displayed by Black males today. Slavery officially ended in December 1865 when the 13th amendment to the Constitution was ratified by the states. However, the abolishment of slavery did not prevent Blacks from experiencing continued discrimination.

Life for Blacks after slavery was similar to undergoing major surgery without receiving anesthesia. Need I say more? Without understating the institution of slavery, we cannot truly understand the psyche of today's Black males. A bad seed was planted and blossomed without appropriate care or intervention. In addition, destructive and inhibiting laws were established to set the stage for continued oppression of Blacks. Black codes were implemented in the 1860s in response to the abolishment of slavery and the South's defeat in the Civil War. The codes were designed to restrict free slaves by providing limited second-class civil rights and no voting rights. This oppressive strategy was an attempt to control Blacks and prevent social equality. Blacks were not allowed to assemble in groups of more than five; own property or testify in court; learn to read or write; conduct religious service without a white person present; strike a white; etc. Black codes made life difficult for Blacks, but fortunately, they were repealed in 1866 after the election of new government officials. What did you learn? How are you feeling? Don't explode. We have only completed the first step of our voyage. Now let's review how the Jim Crow Era contributed to the development of negative emotions possessed by many Blacks males.

Jim Crow Era was a period where Blacks were treated as second class citizens. This era marked the end of Reconstruction to the beginning of the twenty century. Racism was worse during this time period. State and local laws were enacted that mandated de jure segregation in all public facilities. The laws led to treatment and accommodations that were inferior to those provided for white Americans, systematizing a number of economic, educational, and social disadvantages. Blacks could not serve on juries or participate in the justice system or law enforcement. Lynching was widespread and commonly practiced. Blacks were lynched for anything or nothing: stealing, being saucy to white people, being in the wrong place at the wrong time, sleeping with consenting white women, etc. Between 1889 and 1992, the NAACP calculated lynchings reached their worst level in history, almost 3,500 people, almost all of them Black men. What did you learn? Are you informed yet? If no, relax and tighten your seatbelt as we complete our short voyage by reviewing how the Civil Rights Era affected Blacks males.

Civil Rights Era was a reform movement to abolish racial discrimination against Blacks. Brown vs. The Board of Education phased out segregation of schools; the Montgomery Bus Boycott ended segregation of Blacks and Whites on buses; James Meredith entered the campus of Mississippi University; Dr. King gave his famous "I have a Dream" speech in Washington, D.C.; and President Johnson signed the Civil Rights Act into law on July 2, 1964. The Civil Rights Era was a time where Blacks began to rejoice, but their rejoicing was short lived. On August 28, 1955, Emmitt Till was murdered for whistling at a white woman while visiting his uncle in Mississippi. His murderers were acquitted after the jury deliberated for sixty-seven minutes. On February 21, 1965, Malcolm X was murdered in Manhattan before he gave a speech, and Dr. Martin Luther King was assassinated on April 4, 1968 in Memphis after delivering his famous "Mountaintop" sermon. I personally do not believe that Blacks recovered after Dr. King's death. If a man of his demeanor and accomplishment could be

gunned down, how could an ordinary Black man survive?
With the fall of our great spiritual leader, the Black
community digressed, and so did the Black man.

Learning about oppression helped me understand my
pain and defensive posture. I believe that the worst thing in
the world is to experience pain and not understand it; pain
that is passed down from generation to generation; pain that
is so deeply-rooted that it attacks the fabric of your soul.
The pain I felt was the by-product of suffering endured by
Black men throughout history. Let's review.

- Nat Turner (slave and visionary leader) hanged
  1831 in Jerusalem, Virginia
- Between 1889 and 1992, the NAACP calculated
  lynchings reached their worst level in history,
  almost 3,500 people, almost all of them Black men.
- William Brown Lynched 1919 in Douglas County,
  Nebraska
- Lint Shaw Lynched 1936 in Royston, Georgia
- Medgar Wiley Evers murdered 1963 in Jackson,
  Mississippi (age 38)
- James Meredith murdered 1966 in Mississippi (age
  28)
- Rodney King beat severely by police 1991 in
  California (age 24)
- Tupac Shakur (famous rapper) murdered 1996 in
  California (age 25)
- Christopher Wallace A.K.A Biggie Small (famous
  rapper) murdered 1997 in California (age 24)
- Sean Bell murdered 2006 in New York (age 23)
- Jena Six – group of six Black males who were
  charged with beating of a white boy at Jena High
  School in Jena, Louisiana on December 4, 2006.
  Mychal Bell was originally charged with attempted

murder, but the charges were reduced to aggravated battery and conspiracy.

What are your thoughts? Are you suffering from internalized oppression? Has oppression affected you? Before you answer, consider the following: From 2001 to 2005, more than 9 out of 10 black murder victims were killed by other blacks, and three out of four were slain with a gun (Bureau of Justice Statistics). Internalized oppression has penetrated the Black community intensely and has caused Blacks to oppress each other. Black women demean Black men; Black men demean Black women; Black men demean other Black men; and Black women demean other Black women. For decades, oppression has severely handicapped the Black community, especially Black males who, like other men, define their worth by power, status, wealth, and position in society.

Again, I ask, has oppression affected you? Do you have a positive self-concept? Do you have a healthy and uplifting view or perception of yourself? Do treat yourself and others with respect? Do you engage in self-praise? Take responsibility for your choices? Set realistic goals? Focus on positives and strengths and have faith in your abilities? If you answered no to any question, you probably do not have a positive self-concept. A large percentage of Black males do not possess positive self-concepts. Why? Glad you asked. Our self-concepts are usually developed from the views or perceptions held by family, friends, and society. And in my day to day interactions, I often hear others refer to today's Black males as pimps, dogs, gang-bangers, bombs, hustlers, thugs, players, and dead beat dads. Additionally, some black women and whites perceive Black males as being self-centered, selfish, lazy, and violent. While this perception might be true for some, it is not true for all. However, we are all guilty of overgeneralization, and for this reason, I argue that many Black males do not have positive self-concepts. Many see themselves as others see them. This is referred to as social self-concept. As stated previously, oppression has devastated the Black community and Black males. Most are insensitive to the pain of others. Unfortunately, experiencing pain and inflicting it on others is a tragic episodic that has plagued Black males.

Conquering internalized oppression can only be accomplished by understanding it. Your plight is determined by the knowledge you possess. Equipping yourself with proper information is the key to controlling your destiny. In this information age, you have access to resources that our ancestors did not have access to. Ignorance, greed, and selfishness have contained us long enough. It is time to end this modern day slavery. You cannot expect others to do for you what you can do for yourself. As a conqueror and head of your household, you can achieve whatever your heart desires. I believe in you. But more importantly, God believes in you. Do you believe you are capable of conquering internalized oppression? Can you move forward or do you feel inadequate? Do you have a thorough understanding of oppression and how it works? Your comprehension influences what you expect. What do you expect? Are expectations rational? Are your beliefs consistent with your expectations? In the next chapter, we will explore your expectations.

--------------------Be Realistic--------------------

Questions for Reflection and Discussion

Why is it important to understand oppression? (Explain)

Do you believe slavery affected Black males? Yes or No (Explain)

Do you have a positive self-concept? Yes or No (Explain)

Do you treat yourself or others with respect? Yes or No (Explain)

Do you engage in self-praise? Yes or No

Do take responsibility for your actions? Yes or No (Explain)

Do you believe you can conquer internalized oppression? Yes or No (Explain)

What is the first step to conquering internalized oppression?

Use the space below to record your feelings and/or thoughts about this chapter. What did you learn?

*Notes*_____

_____
_____
_____
_____
_____
_____
_____
_____
_____
_____
_____
_____
_____
_____
_____
_____
_____
_____
_____
_____
_____
_____
_____
_____
_____
_____

The significant problems we face cannot be solved at the same level of thinking we were at when we created them.

—Albert Einstein

Develop Rational Expectations

----------- *Chapter 5* -----------

Developing rational expectations is the second strategy to conquering internalized oppression. The expectations you have of yourself and others often reflect how you live your life. Do you live life expecting to fail and hoping to succeed? If you answered yes, it is time to change your expectation.

Expect To Succeed

Expect to succeed and be prepared for failure. Life's disappointments can wear us down and cause us to feel helpless and hopeless. It seems like the more we try to be positive, things get worse, and giving up is the rational thing to do. As a young boy, I was often told that anything that I experienced that did not break me would make me stronger. As a child, I did not understand this concept, but now I can honestly say that I am a better and stronger man because of personal hardships. I learned that my mind is powerful and sets the stage for my performance. If I expect to fail, I perform with fear, no motivation, and doubt. Such emotions are destructive and are highly associated with failure. However, if I expect to succeed, I perform with confidence, enthusiasm, and certainty. The latter emotions are uplifting and are very much linked to success. Shifting your expectations from a failure mentality can lay the foundation for a promising future. Positive thoughts often lead to positive behaviors, thus increasing your chance of succeeding. Life offers no guarantees, but I can guarantee you that if you expect to fail, you probably will (self-fulfilling prophecy).

Examine your expectations or beliefs daily and strive to succeed. A man who believes that he can succeed will expect more and challenge those who offer or expect less of him. Learn to exert yourself and stop living with fear of failing. Failing builds resiliency, and resiliency is a by-product of success. Jesus was perceived to be a failure by those who prosecuted him, but He was successful in accomplishing what He was tasked to do. Failure is professed from the perspective of the assessor, and his or her view may be distorted. Learn to define your own success and do not allow others to define it for you. Success can be defined either by outcome or process. It is important to know and learn the difference. Sometimes we go through things in order to learn a lesson. Although we do not always accomplish our desired outcome, the process can be considered a success if we learn from the experience.

Dwelling on your failure can hold you captive and prevent you from achieving greatness. Well-known scripture figures such as Abraham, Moses, Elijah, David, and Peter experienced failure at some point, but they learned from their failure, confessed it to God, and used it to their advantage to advance His kingdom. They expected to succeed and benefited from God's grace. I encourage you to stop looking to man to help you succeed and ask God. "Ask and you shall receive, seek and you will find; knock and the door will be opened to you; for everyone who asks will receive, and anyone who seeks will find, and the door will be opened to those who knock" (Mathew 7:7-8). If you desire to succeed, turn to the One who can truly help you. **I remind you that everything starts and ends with God. Your desire to succeed is achievable if you ask!**

Expect To Change

You cannot expect your life to improve unless you are willing to change. Doing the same thing over and over and expecting a different outcome is irrational. If you feel oppressed, develop a plan to conquer it. The problems you encounter are partially your fault. Some of you walk around with a chip on your shoulder. You are mad at the world and treat people cruelly, but expect others to treat you fairly. Does this make sense? Also, you expect others to be sensitive to your needs, but you fail to respond sensitively to others. This sense of entitlement is the basis for your madness. Some of you still expect to receive your forty acres and a mule. Not to sound harsh, but no one owes you anything. Stop feeling sorry for yourself. Self-pity usually leads to increased frustration and low motivation. Stop expecting people to meet your needs and strive to meet them yourself. It is totally inappropriate and selfish to degrade others because you are hurting. Your pain might be justified, but it does not give you the right to mistreat others. As the saying goes, misery loves company, especially miserable company. I challenge you to find new company if you are feeling miserable or making others miserable. Changing your environment or the people you socialize with can prove to be beneficial to your well-being.

Expect To Be Informed

Ignorance enslaves many Black males. How do you expect to improve your life or the lives of others, if you lack knowledge? How often do you equip yourself with information that will help you solve or cope with your hardship? Your experience alone is not always the most of effective way of learning. Vernon Law, a famous baseball player, once stated that, "Experience is a hard teacher because she

58

gives the test first, the lesson afterwards." Instead of going through life making mistakes and learning from them, try equipping yourself with proper information before the test.

I often hear brothers talking about changing their situations, but never develop a road map. Is this rational? Traveling the road of life without proper directions or a map can lead to disaster. Matthew 15:14 says, "If the blind lead the blind, both shall fall in the ditch." How can you conquer something you do not understand? Empower yourself by acquiring knowledge and applying it. Lack of knowledge and irrational expectations are the root cause of most irrational emotions and behavior. People perish without knowledge. Can I be blunt? Stop being ignorant!

Expect To Be Generous

If you are privileged to achieve a social status, money, education, or power, please do not walk around with your nose in the air. This mannerism sustains and reinforces oppression. Those who "Have" look down on those who "Have not". Some of you have knocked down barriers to achieve some level of success. And as a result, some of you have developed an "I made it, so can they" attitude. W.E.B. DuBois referred to the "Haves" as the "Talented Tenth". They are the individuals who have achieved success. They are privileged to have nice jobs, drive cars, and live in nice homes. A large percentage is educated and knows what it takes to succeed. DuBois believed that the Talented Tenth was responsible for helping the Non-talented Ninety Percent. But instead of uplifting those who are less fortunate, some of you criticize them or occasionally offer assistance in a snobbish manner. The Talented Tenth neglect to help the Non-Talented Ninety Percent that is left behind. Somehow you forget what it feels like to hurt, suffer, and be discriminated against. Applying their uniqueness to others is commonly practiced among the Talented Tenth. Let me clarify this. Stop expecting others to achieve what you have achieved without carefully taking into account individual differences. Some of you do not realize that you are rare and unique, not the norm. Just look around. How many Blacks hold high positions in organizations or government? Contrary to popular believe, all Blacks are not afforded the same opportunities. Each person was born with a different temperament which influences his/her ability to cope and progress in life. Expecting others to accomplish what you have without knowing their personal situation is irrational. Expect to give back and uplift those who are less fortunate. Giving back is fundamental—somebody helped you! Now, can I flip the script?

If you fall in the "Have Not" category, I encourage you to stop "Hating". Do not envy or covet. You cannot expect people to be generous to you if you are not generous to them. Some of you have too much pride to receive assistance. You also disrespect those who "Have" and talk negative about them. Show your brother or sister some love. Be proud of him/her and extend words of encouragement and support. Expect to be kind, and you are likely to receive it. Life is too short to live it being negative.

Being generous is vital to conquering internalized oppression. Treat others as you would like to be treated. Seek to understand people before you pass judgment. "Judge not, that ye be not judged" (Matthew 7:1).

Expect To Work

God himself worked and expects you to work. According to Genesis 2:15, He placed Adam and Eve in the garden to "tend and keep" it. He created you and me to rule over creation. This requires work. Work is notable and demonstrates faith in God. He promises rewards to people in everyday jobs, based on their attitudes and conduct (Eph 6:7-9, Col 3:23-4:1). We serve a God that cares about our material needs as well as our spiritual needs, and our material needs are met in part by the work we do. Mouths that do not work do not get fed. Work equips you with the things you need and desire. You do not have to depend on others. Self-sufficiency increases your ability to conquer internalized oppression.

As a conqueror and head of your household, you should have high expectations, but not irrational ones. It is a fatal mistake to live life with irrational expectations. Having a clear understanding of why you live your life the way you do is essential to your growth. Do not continue to be victimized by oppression. I realize that our political and social system is not fair, and America has been hard on Black males, but you can help yourself by modifying expectations that make you feel inadequate, inferior, worthless, frustrated, or bitter. I value you and ask you to value yourself. When you feel discouraged, pray and ask God for strength, but do not engage in self-destructive or self-inhibiting behavior. God can and will provide, but you must believe that you can do all things through Christ (Philippians 4:13).

Questions for Reflection and Discussion

Do you live life expecting to fail and hoping to succeed?
Yes or No (Explain)

Do you expect others to be sensitive to your needs, but you
fail to respond sensibly to their? Yes or No (Explain)

Do you equip yourself with knowledge that will enable you
to cope with your hardships more effectively?
Yes or No (Explain)

Are you generous to others who are more or less fortunate
than yourself? Yes or No (Explain)

Do you believe that mouths that do not work should be fed?
Yes or No (Explain)

Why is it important to have rational expectations?

Use the space below to record your feelings and/or thoughts about this chapter. What did you learn?

*Notes*_____

_____

_____

_____

_____

_____

_____

_____

_____

_____

_____

_____

_____

_____

_____

_____

_____

_____

_____

_____

_____

_____

_____

_____

_____

_____

_____

_____

_____

_____

_____

"A warning given by an experienced person to someone willing to listen is more valuable than....jewelry made of the finest gold."

—*Proverbs 25:12*

Maintain a Positive Attitude

----------- *Chapter 6* -----------

Maintaining a positive attitude is the third strategy to conquering internalized oppression. Your way of thinking affects every phase of your life, including your relationships. During my thirty-plus years on this earth, I have experienced many things, and have been in and out of all kinds of relationships. Through those relationships, I have learned that there are two kinds of people: negative thinkers and positive thinkers. Positive thinkers often search for the good in people and situations. They are caring, confident, and respectful of others, as well as themselves. Negative thinkers often search for the bad in people and situations. They are insensitive, unsure, and disrespectful. From the relationships in which I have engaged, I have learned that it is best to be a positive thinker. What do you think?

My life experiences have taught me that I cannot always control what happens to me, but I can control my attitude. It is easy to be negative when you are hurting, discouraged, and angry. Your inner critic makes it easy to criticize yourself, as well as others, especially when your desires or expectations are not met. It is only natural to want to attack those who hurt you, devalue to you, belittle you, or contribute to your oppression. However, fighting fire with fire has never proven to be effective. Negativity leads to negativity. The attitude and behavior you exhibit today will shape your future. Therefore, it is imperative that you explore and change negative attitudes and thoughts. What kind of thinker are you? Do you believe that people are not trustworthy and evil or trustworthy and good?

Freedom from oppression begins with your attitude. Let's review some common distortions of thinking that lead to negative attitudes. Among these distortions are:

Always/never thinking – You think something that happened will "always" recur, or you will "never" secure what you desire or want. For example, if you fail to secure a job you really want, you might think "I always fail and never get what I want". This thought is negative and can cause you to feel inadequate and discouraged.

Blaming – You blame someone else for the hardships in your life, because you see yourself as a victim. You do not accept responsibility for your actions, emotions, or behavior because you feel that others caused them. For example, "I would not be in jail if she would not have called the police. I only hit her because she made me angry. It's her fault."

Blame thinking causes you to feel powerless. "I can't get ahead in life because white people control everything." This kind of thinking restricts you from exercising your personal sense of power. Taking responsibility for your behavior empowers you to change it.

Mental Filter – You select a single negative fact and dwell on it exclusively until your view of reality is gloomy. For example, you receive 9 excellent scores and 1 good score on your performance report. Instead of you being happy about the 9 *excellent* scores, you dwell on the 1 *good* score, telling yourself that you are not good. You have a tendency to filter out anything positive.

Disqualifying the positive – You reject positive experiences by insisting they do not count for some reason or another.

For example, your white boss invites you over for dinner and expresses an interest in getting to know you. But, because you believe that all white people are evil, you do not accept the invitation. This thinking allows you to maintain a negative belief that is contradicted by your everyday experiences.

Jumping to conclusions – You randomly jump to a negative conclusion that is not justified by the facts of the situation. "Mind reading" and "Fortune Teller" are two examples of this kind of thinking.

- o Mind reading – you conclude that someone is reacting negatively to you, and you do not check the facts. "I never talked to her, but I know she does not like me because she does not speak."

- o Fortune Teller – you anticipate that things will turn out poorly, and you feel convinced that your prediction is an already established fact. "Why should I try to connect with people I do not like or know? It will be a disaster."

Emotional reasoning – You assume that your negative emotions automatically reflect the way things really are. "I feel it, therefore it must be true. I feel inadequate, therefore my problems must be impossible to solve."

Labeling and Mislabeling – Instead of describing your mistake, you attach a negative label to yourself. "I'm a loser." When someone else's behavior rubs you the wrong way, you attach a negative label to him. "He's a loser." Mislabeling – You describe an event with language that is highly distorted and emotionally loaded. "I'm a failure" instead of "I made a mistake".

Personalization – You see yourself as the cause of some negative external event which, in fact, you were not primarily responsible for. This distortion is the primary cause of feeling guilty. For example, "It's my fault that my daughter got pregnant. I did not talk to her about safe sex; it's my fault that my son was arrested. We should have moved out of the neighborhood."

Are you guilty of using any of the distortions listed above? You are responsible for your attitude. Your view on life depends upon what you tell yourself, how you treat yourself, and how you understand your world. Your suffering can be intensified or relieved by your attitude.

It is important to pay attention to your attitude, especially negative attitudes that affect your relationships, work, and life in general. Recognizing and modifying negative attitudes early is the most effective way of reducing their impact. If you fail to address negative attitudes early, you begin to believe them, and inappropriate behavior follows. While it is normal to protect yourself from being hurt or oppressed, it is unhealthy to maintain negative attitudes. But, unfortunately, most of us struggle to remove negative attitudes because they are deeply rooted in our belief systems. Sometimes we are being negative, yet are not aware. For this reason, it is important to check your attitude before you respond to a situation or person. By now you might be asking, "What does my attitude have to do with oppression?" I am glad you asked.

Negative attitudes are often used to justify the subordination, marginalization, and silencing of other individuals' oppression. Disempowering people because you feel they are inferior is all about attitude. Some men abuse their women and children because they believe they are inferior or powerless. Some men sleep with multiple women because they do not respect or think highly of women. Negative attitudes and oppression go hand-in-hand. Over time, people who oppress others become increasingly negative and cold. People start avoiding them or treating them how they treat others. Maintaining a positive attitude of yourself and others is critical to conquering internalized oppression. When you view yourself and others in a positive manner, it makes it easier for others to respect and bond with you.

Maintain a Positive Attitude

Unfortunately, as a result of harsh experiences, some of you find it is difficult to maintain a positive attitude. The inner negative critic tells you to screw the world and the people in it. The internal anguish caused by this thinking makes you behave in a negative way that distances others, thus reinforcing your desire to distance yourself.

Men and young boys who go through life with negative attitudes are at greater risk of becoming victims of oppression or oppressing others. Learn to replace negative attitudes with positive attitudes:

Negative Attitudes:

- Violent
- Rude
- Ungrateful
- Judgmental
- Insensitive
- Unsure
- Incompetent
- Unskilled
- Pessimistic
- Narrow-minded
- Non-talented

Positive Attitudes:

- Peaceful
- Polite
- Thankful
- Non-judgmental
- Compassionate
- Confident
- Competent
- Optimistic
- Open-minded
- Self-controlled
- Talented

Maintaining a positive attitude is achievable and can help you view yourself and others optimistically. To successfully maintain a positive attitude, you must adjust your thinking. Effectively applying the seven strategies below will enable you live a joyful and victorious life.

1.)   **Identify distortions** in your thinking. Faulty thinking in unhealthy for you. Identifying negative attitudes is the first step to maintaining a positive attitude.

_____

_____

_____

_____

_____

_____

2.) **Counter your inner critic** by challenging the negative inner voice that attacks and judges you and others. Frequent monitoring of your inner critic prevents distortions from manifesting.

_____
_____
_____
_____
_____
_____

3.) **Identify your strengths** and establish an accurate list of them and your resources. Review your list daily to remind yourself of your strengths.

_____
_____
_____
_____
_____
_____

4.) **Use thought stopping.** When the inner critic attacks aggressively, stop the negative thinking and revisit healthy thoughts.

_____
_____
_____
_____
_____
_____

72

5.) **Accept yourself and others without passing judgment.** Deal with facts only and eliminate negative emotions.

_____
_____
_____
_____
_____
_____

6.) **Avoid being passive and inflexible.** Express your emotions assertively and be open to feedback and change.

_____
_____
_____
_____
_____
_____

7.) **Reinforce healthy self-talk.** Use positive affirmations to reinforce healthy self-talk. Examples: "I will surround myself with positive individuals and ideas; and I will not give up until I achieve the result I desire."

_____
_____
_____
_____
_____
_____

Maintaining and fostering a positive attitude requires you to be diverse in your thinking. It is important to learn alternative viewpoints. It is also important to understand yourself. You are your worst critic. What you feel or tell yourself is not always true or accurate. Looking for the good in yourself and others should become a habit. A habit is a point where desire, knowledge, and skill meet. Take time to learn about other people by being active, looking for common ground, assuming differences in meaning, and looking for individuals, not group representatives. Doing the latter will enable you to maintain a positive attitude. Be mindful that maintaining a positive attitude of yourself and others does not guarantee that your life or situation will change. However, it cannot make it worse either. If nothing changes, at least you feel better. **Do not allow your negative attitude to rob you of the happiness you deserve!**

Questions for Reflection and Discussion

Why is it important to maintain a positive attitude?
(Explain)

What does negativity lead to?

Can a negative or self-defeating attitude cause you to suffer
from oppression or oppress others?

What are some common cognitive distortions that cause
negative thinking?

What can you do to maintain a positive attitude?

Who controls how you think and feel?

Use the space below to record your feelings and/or thoughts about this chapter. What did you learn?

*Notes*_____

_____
_____
_____
_____
_____
_____
_____
_____
_____
_____
_____
_____
_____
_____
_____
_____
_____
_____
_____
_____
_____
_____
_____
_____
_____
_____
_____

--------------------A Black Man's Worth!---------------------

Nonviolence is the answer to the crucial political and moral questions of our time: the need for man to overcome oppression and violence without resorting to oppression and violence. Man must evolve for all human conflict a method which rejects revenge, aggression, and retaliation. The foundation of such a method is love.

—Martin Luther King Jr.

Love Unconditionally

---------- *Chapter 7* ----------

Loving unconditionally is the fourth strategy to conquering internalized oppression. Do you know how to love? Do you know what it means to love someone unconditionally? Do you struggle to love others at times? Before you answer these questions, I challenge you to think about your definition of love and examine your source. Who or what shaped your view about love? What does love mean to you?

According to the Wikipedia, the word love can refer to a variety of different feelings, states, and attitudes, ranging from generic pleasure to intense interpersonal attraction. Many people define love as a strong, intense, and indescribable feeling towards another person or group of people. However, due to individual and culture differences, it is too difficult, if not impossible, to establish a universal definition of love. I truly believe that many of us go through life feeling deprived of love because we were equipped improperly. Many of us were conditioned to believe that love can be earned by doing good deeds; conditioned to believe that we should only love those who love us; and conditioned to believe that love does not hurt.

Although the nature or essence of love is a subject of frequent debate, the meaning and application of it can be clarified by studying the ***Word***. Your ability to love yourself and others unconditionally is challenging, because you do not know what true love is. And you often look in the wrong places. The heart of God and the gospel of Christ is love.

Love is compassion, grace, sacrifice, and mercy. Yes, compassion, sacrifice, and mercy! Sometimes you have to be willing to give up someone or something you love to demonstrate compassion for others. God sacrificed his only begotten Son to show us how much He loves us. In addition, He continues to show love for us despite our wrongdoing. Loving others, like God loves us, can be difficult, but conquering internalized oppression will not occur until you learn to love as He does. It is easy to fall victim to loving others based on conditions. However, I am delighted that God does not love us based on conditions because we all have fallen short of His glory.

We are all cohorts on our journey to reach heaven, and our greatest challenge is loving ourselves and others unconditionally. How can we overcome this challenge? The first step is to love without forcing our rules, requirements, and conditions on others. Let me explain! God loves us so much that He allows us to do as we please. He does not force His love on us or remove it based on our actions. It is true that He has rules for His children and expects us to follow them. But He loves us unlimitedly. He permits us to make mistakes and continues to love us even if He does not approve of our behavior. His compassion for us is immeasurable. He is merciful to those who wrong Him or disobey Him. He does not force us to change. Instead, He provides a firsthand lesson on how to love unconditionally. He teaches how to love daily and never forsakes us. His love is love without conditions. Do you know what this means?

To love unconditionally, you must allow others to exercise their Free Will. Yes! It is your responsibility to lead your household; and Yes! It is your responsibility to educate and challenge those who oppress you. But remember, you cannot control them. Understanding the difference between control and influence will enable you to love unconditionally. **Control** means to master or command, and ***influence*** is the act or power of producing an effect without obvious application of force or direct exercise of command. As mentioned earlier, God does not force us to love Him, and He does not withhold his love. At this point, you are probably wondering how this applies to you.

One of the major problems that you have developed is withholding your love to control others. You have made known to your wife, children, and others that if they behave or perform in a certain way, you will withdraw your love. Is this behavior Godly? God commands us to love others without limiting their ability or freedom to exercise their Free Will. I realize that this is a difficult task, especially in regards to our children. As a parent, it is your duty to teach your children right from wrong as early as possible. Give them choices and explain the consequences. Provide them with as much information as possible to make good decisions, but do not force your thoughts or solutions on them. Your job is to influence their behavior and let them know that you will love them unconditionally regardless of what they decide. This is what God does. He is present always and loves you when you are sick or healthy; happy or sad; obedient or disobedient. He loves us enough to give us total freedom. He wants us to love him by choice, not by force. When you love someone unconditionally, and they know it, all doubt, fear, and anxiety is removed from their heart. I strongly encourage you to apply this principle in your marriage and relationships. *Love to influence, not to control.*

God instructs us to love others despite their behavior, appearance, background, economic, social, or financial status. Inflicting pain on others, or holding grudges and hatred against your oppressors, will never free you from the shackles of oppression. Loving unconditionally is God's remedy to conquering internalized oppression. At times you might question your ability to love your offenders, but once you let go, all the harsh emotions and turmoil will disappear from life. Would you like to experience love like this? Do you believe it is humanly possible to love unconditionally?

I hope you answered yes! God created you in his likeness and blessed you with the gift of love. All you must do is apply what's in your heart. Do you believe? Let's explore four heartfelt strategies you can implement to learn to love others as well as yourself unconditionally.

1. Love like God
2. Understand Love
3. Have Compassion
4. Be Forgiving

Strategy 1: Love like God. God's love is total, says Paul. It reaches every corner of our experience. It is wide; it covers the breadth of our own experience, and reaches out to the whole world. God's love is long; it continues the length of our lives. It is high; it rises to the heights of our celebration and elation. His love is deep; – it reaches to the depth of discouragement, despair, and even death (Ephesians 3:17-19).

Strategy 2: Understand Love. Love is not hate; Love is not resentful; Love is not conditional; Love is not pride; Love is not limited; Love is not a gift from man; Love is not to be taken for granted; Love is not restricted to a specific race or gender. Let me be clear, love is God.

Strategy 3: Have Compassion for others. Do you know the difference between sympathy and compassion? Sympathy means to feel sorry for someone, but it does not require you to do anything. Compassion, on the other hand, means to feel sympathetic to other's pain, but it requires

82

actions. An individual who is compassionate takes actions to relieve others of their suffering. A compassionate person does what is right even in difficult times. When no one else will step up, a compassionate person does. This is what Jesus did for us. A compassionate person does not judge others; instead, he or she helps when warranted. To have a relationship with Jesus and live a Christ-like lifestyle, you must have compassion for others. Compassion fulfills the law of Christ (Galatians 6:2).

Strategy 4: Be Forgiving. Forgiving others is not easy, but God requires you to. If you desire forgiveness, you must be willing to forgive. Refusing to forgive others is a sign of selfishness. God is not selfish, so He expects you to forgive others.

I know it feels unfair to forgive individuals who have abused you, neglected, embarrassed you, belittled you, oppressed you, molested you, or took the life of your loved one, but forgiveness will enable you to heal. Letting go of anger and hatred is healthy for you and uplifts God's family. Forgiveness is a Godly obligation. In addition, forgiveness empowers you to take control over your emotions. As long as you harbor unforgiveness, you are empowering those who hurt you. When you release harsh feelings, you allow God's forgiveness to downpour into your life.

Finally, keep in mind that forgiveness is a negative emotion that handicaps you. If you walk around holding grudges, you will deprive yourself of God's blessings. Some individuals will offend you, then go home and sleep like a baby. For this reason, you must let go and move on. Remember that no one is perfect. Each one of us has offended others, so it is important to forgive others so God can forgive you. Pray for those who hurt you because they are hurting themselves. Those who hurt you are probably intimidated by you, jealous of you, or afraid of you. If it is possible and safe, seek to understand their rage; remove yourself from the situation and pray for them.

Do not permit others to strip you of your gift of love. God created you out of love so you can love yourself and others. Don't be afraid to love yourself and others unconditionally. The benefits can be great depending on your attitude. Nelson Mandela glorified the importance of loving yourself and living without fear by stating, "And as we let our light shine, we unconsciously give other people permission to do the same. As we're liberated from our own fear, our presence automatically liberates others."

Where Do I Go From Here?

To love unconditionally, practice the strategies listed above daily, share your love with others, and use the following poem for inspiration:

Foolish is he who is afraid to let love in.

Allow love to surround and embrace you with all that it has. Allow yourself to be loved, to feel love, to give love.

Do not push love aside. Do not hide your love!

Just stand back and allow your heart to show you love.

For it is better to have loved and lost it, then never to have loved at all.

Take all love and learn from it, experiment with it, but don't play with it.

For love is not a toy or merely a four-letter word.

Love is an emotion, a feeling and desire from within.

Appreciate every moment of it.

Take from love everything you possibly can.

For you may never be able to love again.

In doing all these things, and only then, will you know what true love really is.

—Diana

"Apply Strategies"

Identify a person or group of people that you are having difficulty loving unconditionally and apply the strategies to recondition your heart.

Strategy 1: Love like God

_____
_____
_____
_____
_____
_____
_____

Strategy 2: Understand Love

_____
_____
_____
_____
_____
_____
_____

Strategy 3: Have Compassion

_____
_____
_____
_____
_____
_____
_____

Strategy 4: Be Merciful – Forgive

_____

_____

_____

_____

_____

_____

_____

Questions for Reflection and Discussion

Do you struggle to love others at times? Yes or No (Explain)

Do you know what it means to love unconditionally? Yes or No (Explain)

Who or what shaped your view of love?

What is love to you? What does unconditional mean to you?

Is God's love unconditional? Yes or No

How does God demonstrate his unconditional love for us? (Explain)

What strategies can you use to love yourself and others unconditionally?

--------------------A Black Man's Worth!--------------------

88

Use the space below to record your feelings and/or thoughts about this chapter. What did you learn?

*Notes*_____

_____
_____
_____
_____
_____
_____
_____
_____
_____
_____
_____
_____
_____
_____
_____
_____
_____
_____
_____
_____
_____
_____
_____
_____
_____
_____
_____

--------------------Love Unconditionally--------------------

An unfriendly man pursues selfish ends; he defies all sound judgment.

—Proverbs 18:1

Conclusion

As a brother, I understand your struggle to conquer internalized oppression and conduct yourself like a R.E.A.L. man. On a daily basis, you have to deal with racism, inequality, and economic oppression, while trying to care for yourself and your family. Coping with this harsh reality is not easy. Oppression has caused many of us to believe that we are not important. We are constantly trying to prove ourselves, and this can be very stressful. This hindrance is something that I have experienced personally. Traumatic early-life experiences have led many of us to abandon our God-given identity to take on the identity given to us by our oppressors. We have learned to feel inferior and dispensable. And we have spent our entire lives living with and defending identities we were traumatized into accepting.

Do you remember how you saw the world through the innocent and loving eyes of a child before you were hurt by the harsh realities of being a Black male in America? You were pure as a child. You believed that love could conquer all. You believed in others and in yourself.

I challenge you to revisit the child in you. You were not afraid to express how you felt. You were not afraid to love. You were not afraid to cry. You did not mind helping or running errands for others. You showed pride in helping others in need. You smiled when others smiled at you. You experienced and expressed joy and happiness. Do you believe you could ever experience what you felt as a child again? I believe you can! Is this being realistic? It depends

92

on your viewpoint. From a worldly viewpoint, I would say no. But from a Godly viewpoint, I would say yes. 1 Corinthians 13:11 states, "When I was a child, I spoke as a child, I understood as a child, I thought as a child; but when I became a man, I put away childish things." Let me explain what this means to me. I thought I could define meaning for my own life, and I engaged in childish behavior, but after I acquired proper knowledge regarding the meaning of my life, I stopped being childish. I changed my thoughts and behavior, but not my childish heart. A heart that initially enabled me to see the world through God's eyes! Eyes that see good people and love! Remember that your view on life determines how you live it. Maintain a childish heart, but conduct yourself as a R.E.A.L. man. Be realistic, have rational expectations, maintain a positive attitude, and love unconditionally.

Reclaiming your uncontaminated identity and conquering internalized oppression can be accomplished by restoring and enhancing your spiritual relationship with God. Through God all things are possible. As you re-connect with God, you become free from the shackles of oppression. This does not mean that you will not continue to experience oppression, because others are liberated to use their Free Will as they see fit, but it does means that you will be better equipped to cope with it. I hope that I have inspired you to become the R.E.A.L. man that you can be. I pray that you acquire and accomplish all that your heart desires. Remember that your purpose in life is to do God's Will. For your obedience, you will reap the benefits of His kingdom.

Appendix 1

A Black Man's Self-Empowerment Creed!

I can no longer blame others for my plight.

My view of myself will influence how others respond to and treat me.

I am responsible for my actions and will take full responsibility for them, while holding others accountable as well.

I can cope with adversity productively, without feeling sad and making excuses for myself.

I will make an effort to address racism and discrimination and challenge all stereotypes that degrade my character.

I realize that I cannot change my past, but I can influence my future!

Wherever the mind goes the body will follow!

Dwayne L. Buckingham

Appendix 2

A Helper's Creed!!

I will examine how I view Black males.

I will express empathy, not sympathy, in my attempt to help and understand Black males.

I will hold Black males accountable for their actions while modeling expression of positive and healthy emotions.

I will not reinforce negative perceptions of Blacks and will challenge those who do.

I will remind Black males of their strengths and promote a can-do attitude.

I can't expect a Black man to cope with and solve his hardships alone, and I will exemplify compassion and sincerity to help!

Behind every action there is an emotion!

Dwayne L. Buckingham

--------------------A Black Man's Worth!--------------------

Appendix 3

Dr. Martin Luther King, Jr.

I Have a Dream
—Delivered at the Lincoln Memorial on August 28, 1963

I am happy to join with you today in what will go down in history as the greatest demonstration for freedom in the history of our nation.

Five score years ago, a great American, in whose symbolic shadow we stand today, signed the Emancipation Proclamation. This momentous decree came as a great beacon light of hope to millions of Negro slaves who had been seared in the flames of withering injustice. It came as a joyous daybreak to end the long night of their captivity.

But one hundred years later, the Negro still is not free. One hundred years later, the life of the Negro is still sadly crippled by the manacles of segregation and the chains of discrimination. One hundred years later, the Negro lives on a lonely island of poverty in the midst of a vast ocean of material prosperity. One hundred years later, the Negro is still languished in the corners of American society and finds himself an exile in his own land. And so we've come here today to dramatize a shameful condition.

In a sense we've come to our nation's capital to cash a check. When the architects of our republic wrote the magnificent words of the Constitution and the Declaration of Independence, they were signing a promissory note to which every American was to fall heir. This note was a promise that all men, yes, black men as well as white men, would be guaranteed the "unalienable Rights" of "Life, Liberty and the pursuit of Happiness." It is obvious today that America has defaulted on this promissory note, insofar as her citizens of color are concerned. Instead of honoring this sacred obligation, America has given the Negro people a bad check, a check which has come back marked "insufficient funds."

But we refuse to believe that the bank of justice is bankrupt. We refuse to believe that there are insufficient funds in the great vaults of opportunity of this nation. And so, we've come to cash this check, a check that will give us upon demand the riches of freedom and the security of justice.

We have also come to this hallowed spot to remind America of the fierce urgency of Now. This is no time to engage in the luxury of cooling off or to take the tranquilizing drug of gradualism. Now is the time to make real the promises of democracy. Now is the time to rise from the dark and desolate valley of segregation to the sunlit path of racial justice. Now is the time to lift our nation from the quick sands of racial injustice to the solid rock of brotherhood. Now is the time to make justice a reality for all of God's children.

It would be fatal for the nation to overlook the urgency of the moment. This sweltering summer of the Negro's legitimate discontent will not pass until there is an invigorating autumn of freedom and equality. Nineteen sixty-three is not an end, but a beginning. And those who hope that the Negro needed to blow off steam and will now be content will have a rude awakening if the nation returns to business as usual. And there will be neither rest nor tranquility in America until the Negro is granted his citizenship rights. The whirlwinds of revolt will continue to shake the foundations of our nation until the bright day of justice emerges.

But there is something that I must say to my people, who stand on the warm threshold which leads into the palace of justice: In the process of gaining our rightful place, we must not be guilty of wrongful deeds. Let us not seek to satisfy our thirst for freedom by drinking from the cup of bitterness and hatred. We must forever conduct our struggle on the high plane of dignity and discipline. We must not allow our creative protest to degenerate into physical violence. Again and again, we must rise to the majestic heights of meeting physical force with soul force.

The marvelous new militancy which has engulfed the Negro community must not lead us to a distrust of all white people, for many of our white brothers, as evidenced by their presence here today, have come to realize that their destiny is tied up with our destiny. And they have come to realize that their freedom is inextricably bound to our freedom.

--------------------A Black Man's Worth!--------------------

We cannot walk alone.

And as we walk, we must make the pledge that we shall always march ahead.

We cannot turn back.

There are those who are asking the devotees of civil rights, "When will you be satisfied?" We can never be satisfied as long as the Negro is the victim of the unspeakable horrors of police brutality. We can never be satisfied as long as our bodies, heavy with the fatigue of travel, cannot gain lodging in the motels of the highways and the hotels of the cities. *We cannot be satisfied as long as the negro's basic mobility is from a smaller ghetto to a larger one. We can never be satisfied as long as our children are stripped of their self-hood and robbed of their dignity by a sign stating: "For Whites Only."* We cannot be satisfied as long as a Negro in Mississippi cannot vote and a Negro in New York believes he has nothing for which to vote. No, no, we are not satisfied, and we will not be satisfied until "justice rolls down like waters, and righteousness like a mighty stream."[1]

I am not unmindful that some of you have come here out of great trials and tribulations. Some of you have come fresh from narrow jail cells. And some of you have come from areas where your quest – quest for freedom – left you battered by the storms of persecution and staggered by the winds of police brutality. You have been the veterans of creative suffering. Continue to work with the faith that unearned suffering is redemptive. Go back to Mississippi, go back to Alabama, go back to South Carolina, go back to Georgia, go back to Louisiana, go back to the slums and ghettos of our northern cities, knowing that somehow this situation can and will be changed.

Let us not wallow in the valley of despair, I say to you today, my friends.

And so even though we face the difficulties of today and tomorrow, I still have a dream. It is a dream deeply rooted in the American dream.

I have a dream that one day this nation will rise up and live out the true meaning of its creed: "We hold these truths to be self-evident, that all men are created equal."

I have a dream that one day on the red hills of Georgia, the sons of former slaves and the sons of former slave owners will be able to sit down together at the table of brotherhood.

I have a dream that one day even the state of Mississippi, a state sweltering with the heat of injustice, sweltering with the heat of oppression, will be transformed into an oasis of freedom and justice.

I have a dream that my four little children will one day live in a nation where they will not be judged by the color of their skin but by the content of their character.

I have a *dream* today!

I have a dream that one day, down in Alabama, with its vicious racists, with its governor having his lips dripping with the words of "interposition" and "nullification" – one day right there in Alabama little black boys and black girls will be able to join hands with little white boys and white girls as sisters and brothers.

---------------------A Black Man's Worth!---------------------

I have a *dream* today!

I have a dream that one day every valley shall be exalted, and every hill and mountain shall be made low, the rough places will be made plain, and the crooked places will be made straight; "and the glory of the Lord shall be revealed and all flesh shall see it together."[2]

This is our hope, and this is the faith that I go back to the South with.

With this faith, we will be able to hew out of the mountain of despair a stone of hope. With this faith, we will be able to transform the jangling discords of our nation into a beautiful symphony of brotherhood. With this faith, we will be able to work together, to pray together, to struggle together, to go to jail together, to stand up for freedom together, knowing that we will be free one day.

And this will be the day – this will be the day when all of God's children will be able to sing with new meaning:

My country 'tis of thee, sweet land of liberty, of thee I sing.

Land where my fathers died, land of the Pilgrim's pride,

From every mountainside, let freedom ring!

And if America is to be a great nation, this must become true.

And so let freedom ring from the prodigious hilltops of New Hampshire.

--------------------A Black Man's Worth!--------------------

Let freedom ring from the mighty mountains of New York.

Let freedom ring from the heightening Alleghenies of Pennsylvania.

Let freedom ring from the snow-capped Rockies of Colorado.

Let freedom ring from the curvaceous slopes of California.

But not only that:

Let freedom ring from Stone Mountain of Georgia.

Let freedom ring from Lookout Mountain of Tennessee.

Let freedom ring from every hill and molehill of Mississippi.

From every mountainside, let freedom ring.

And when this happens, when we allow freedom ring, when we let it ring from every village and every hamlet, from every state and every city, we will be able to speed up that day when *all* of God's children, black men and white men, Jews and Gentiles, Protestants and Catholics, will be able to join hands and sing in the words of the old Negro spiritual:

Free at last! Free at last!

Thank God Almighty, we are free at last!

President Barack Obama

Victory Speech

—Delivered at Grant Park in Chicago, Illinois on November 5, 2008

If there is anyone out there who still doubts that America is a place where all things are possible; who still wonders if the dream of our founders is alive in our time; who still questions the power of our democracy, tonight is your answer.

It's the answer told by lines that stretched around schools and churches in numbers this nation has never seen; by people who waited three hours and four hours, many for the very first time in their lives, because they believed that this time must be different; that their voice could be that difference.

It's the answer spoken by young and old, rich and poor, Democrat and Republican, black, white, Latino, Asian, Native American, gay, straight, disabled and not disabled –

---------------------A Black Man's Worth!---------------------

Americans who sent a message to the world that we have never been a collection of Red States and Blue States: we are, and always will be, the United States of America.

It's the answer that led those who have been told for so long by so many to be cynical, and fearful, and doubtful of what we can achieve to put their hands on the arc of history and bend it once more toward the hope of a better day.

It's been a long time coming, but tonight, because of what we did on this day, in this election, at this defining moment, change has come to America.

I just received a very gracious call from Senator McCain. He fought long and hard in this campaign, and he's fought even longer and harder for the country he loves. He has endured sacrifices for America that most of us cannot begin to imagine, and we are better off for the service rendered by this brave and selfless leader. I congratulate him and Governor Palin for all they have achieved, and I look forward to working with them to renew this nation's promise in the months ahead.

I want to thank my partner in this journey, a man who campaigned from his heart and spoke for the men and women he grew up with on the streets of Scranton and rode with on that train home to Delaware, the Vice President-elect of the United States, Joe Biden.

I would not be standing here tonight without the unyielding support of my best friend for the last sixteen years, the rock of our family and the love of my life, our nation's next First Lady, Michelle Obama. Sasha and Malia, I love you both so much, and you have earned the new puppy that's coming with us to the White House. And while she's no longer with us, I know my grandmother is watching, along with the family that made me who I am. I miss them tonight, and know that my debt to them is beyond measure.

To my campaign manager David Plouffe, my chief strategist David Axelrod, and the best campaign team ever assembled in the history of politics – you made this happen, and I am forever grateful for what you've sacrificed to get it done.

But above all, I will never forget who this victory truly belongs to – it belongs to you.

I was never the likeliest candidate for this office. We didn't start with much money or many endorsements. Our campaign was not hatched in the halls of Washington – it began in the backyards of Des Moines and the living rooms of Concord and the front porches of Charleston.

It was built by working men and women who dug into what little savings they had to give five dollars and ten dollars and twenty dollars to this cause. It grew strength from the young people who rejected the myth of their generation's apathy; who left their homes and their families for jobs that offered little pay and less sleep; from the not-so-young people who braved the bitter cold and scorching heat to knock on the doors of perfect strangers; from the millions of Americans who volunteered, and organized, and proved that more than two centuries later, a government of the people, by the people and for the people has not perished from this Earth. This is your victory.

I know you didn't do this just to win an election and I know you didn't do it for me. You did it because you understand the enormity of the task that lies ahead. For even as we celebrate tonight, we know the challenges that tomorrow will bring are the greatest of our lifetime – two wars, a planet in peril, the worst financial crisis in a century. Even as we stand here tonight, we know there are brave Americans waking up in the deserts of Iraq and the mountains of Afghanistan to risk their lives for us. There are mothers and fathers who will lie awake after their children fall asleep and wonder how they'll make the mortgage, or pay their doctor's bills, or save enough for college. There is new energy to harness and new jobs to be created; new schools to build and threats to meet and alliances to repair.

The road ahead will be long. Our climb will be steep. We may not get there in one year or even one term, but America – I have never been more hopeful than I am tonight that we will get there. I promise you – we as a people will get there.

There will be setbacks and false starts. There are many who won't agree with every decision or policy I make as President, and we know that government can't solve every problem. But I will always be honest with you about the challenges we face. I will listen to you, especially when we disagree. And above all, I will ask you join in the work of remaking this nation the only way it's been done in America for two-hundred and twenty-one years – block by block, brick by brick, calloused hand by calloused hand.

What began twenty-one months ago in the depths of winter must not end on this autumn night. This victory alone is not the change we seek – it is only the chance for us to make that change. And that cannot happen if we go back to the way things were. It cannot happen without you.

So let us summon a new spirit of patriotism; of service and responsibility where each of us resolves to pitch in and work harder and look after not only ourselves, but each other. Let us remember that if this financial crisis taught us anything, it's that we cannot have a thriving Wall Street while Main Street suffers – in this country, we rise or fall as one nation; as one people.

Let us resist the temptation to fall back on the same partisanship and pettiness and immaturity that has poisoned our politics for so long. Let us remember that it was a man from this state who first carried the banner of the Republican Party to the White House – a party founded on the values of self-reliance, individual liberty, and national unity. Those are values we all share, and while the Democratic Party has won a great victory tonight, we do so with a measure of humility and determination to heal the divides that have held back our progress. As Lincoln said to a nation far more divided than ours, "We are not enemies, but friends…though passion may have strained it must not break our bonds of affection." And to those Americans whose support I have yet to earn – I may not have won your vote, but I hear your voices, I need your help, and I will be your President too.

And to all those watching tonight from beyond our shores, from parliaments and palaces to those who are huddled around radios in the forgotten corners of our world – our stories are singular, but our destiny is shared, and a new dawn of American leadership is at hand. To those who would tear this world down – we will defeat you. To those who seek peace and security – we support you. And to all those who have wondered if America's beacon still burns as bright – tonight we proved once more that the true strength of our nation comes not from our the might of our arms or the scale of our wealth, but from the enduring power of our ideals: democracy, liberty, opportunity, and unyielding hope.

For that is the true genius of America – that America can change. Our union can be perfected. And what we have already achieved gives us hope for what we can and must achieve tomorrow.

This election had many firsts and many stories that will be told for generations. But one that's on my mind tonight is about a woman who cast her ballot in Atlanta. She's a lot like the millions of others who stood in line to make their voice heard in this election except for one thing – Ann Nixon Cooper is 106 years old.

She was born just a generation past slavery; a time when there were no cars on the road or planes in the sky; when someone like her couldn't vote for two reasons – because she was a woman and because of the color of her skin.

And tonight, I think about all that she's seen throughout her century in America – the heartache and the hope; the struggle and the progress; the times we were told that we can't, and the people who pressed on with that American creed: Yes we can.

At a time when women's voices were silenced and their hopes dismissed, she lived to see them stand up and speak out and reach for the ballot. Yes we can.

When there was despair in the dust bowl and depression across the land, she saw a nation conquer fear itself with a New Deal, new jobs and a new sense of common purpose. Yes we can.

When the bombs fell on our harbor and tyranny threatened the world, she was there to witness a generation rise to greatness and a democracy was saved. Yes we can.

She was there for the buses in Montgomery, the hoses in Birmingham, a bridge in Selma, and a preacher from Atlanta who told a people that "We Shall Overcome." Yes we can.

A man touched down on the moon, a wall came down in Berlin, a world was connected by our own science and imagination. And this year, in this election, she touched her finger to a screen, and cast her vote, because after 106 years in America, through the best of times and the darkest of hours, she knows how America can change. Yes we can.

America, we have come so far. We have seen so much. But there is so much more to do. So tonight, let us ask ourselves – if our children should live to see the next century; if my daughters should be so lucky to live as long as Ann Nixon Cooper, what change will they see? What progress will we have made?

This is our chance to answer that call. This is our moment. This is our time – to put our people back to work and open doors of opportunity for our kids; to restore prosperity and promote the cause of peace; to reclaim the American Dream and reaffirm that fundamental truth – that out of many, we are one; that while we breathe, we hope, and where we are met with cynicism, and doubt, and those who tell us that we can't, we will respond with that timeless creed that sums up the spirit of a people:

Yes We Can.

Thank you, God bless you, and may God Bless the United States of America.

Appendix 4

R.E.A.L. BLACK Men

Life as a Black male is difficult, but many have laid a foundation and established a legacy that has made it easier for Black males to fight against discrimination, oppression, and exploitation. A world without influential Black men like Fredrick Douglass, Thurgood Marshall, Martin Luther King, Jr., and Barack Obama would be a world without pride, strength, resiliency, hope, and change. They define perseverance and have elevated the Black community, while also helping millions understand and appreciate the true character of Black males. They are the heart of America and the soul of the Black community. Without question, they were and are R.E.A.L Black men.

(Biographical information listed below was taken from Aboutus.com: African-American History and was written by Jessica McElrath)

BARACK OBAMA
(August 4, 1961 – Present)

Occupation: First Black President of the United States of America

Barack Hussein Obama was born in Honolulu, Hawaii on August 4, 1961. Obama is the son of Barack Obama Sr. from Kenya, and a white mother, Ann Dunham, from Kansas. Both of his parents are now deceased.

110

The couple met while they were studying at the East-West Center of the University of Hawaii at Manca. They later married. Their marriage was short; when Obama was two years old, his parents divorced. His father left Hawaii to pursue his Ph.D. at Harvard, and later returned to Kenya. Obama did see his father again when he was ten years old.

His mother's second marriage to Indonesian born Lolo Soetoro resulted in Obama and his mother's move to Jakarta in 1967. His mother and Soetoro had a daughter together. When Obama was ten years old, he returned to Hawaii to live with his grandparents; his mother later joined him. He attended the prestigious prep school Punahou Academy, graduating in 1978.

Obama was raised by his mother and paternal grandparents. Although in his immediate family, he had less connection to his black origins; his own reflections on his childhood reveal his keen sense about prejudice and the racial divide in America. By the time he was a teenager, his sensibilities led him on an exploration of his own racial identity; he was drawn to the works of Langston Hughes, W.E.B. Du Bois, James Baldwin, and Malcolm X's autobiography. Obama came to identify himself as African American despite his biracial heritage. According to Obama, "I self-identify as African American; that's how I'm treated and that's how I'm viewed. I'm proud of it."

After graduating from high school, Obama moved to Los Angeles where he attended Occidental College for two years before transferring to Columbia University. He graduated with a degree in political science in 1983. Obama briefly worked at Business International Corporation and NYPRIG, but ultimately decided on a more altruistic line of work. In

1985, he moved to Chicago and began working as a community organizer for a group of churches.

It was in Chicago, during his work with community pastors, that Obama began to delve into the Christian faith. As a child, Obama had been exposed to Catholicism and the Muslim faith while in Indonesia, as well as other religions during his childhood, but his mother had not raised him to believe in any particular religion. Obama found that, unlike his mother, he had a desire to become part of a community of faith. It was the African American religious tradition of working toward social change that cemented his move toward membership in Chicago's Trinity United Church of Christ.

In 1988, Obama left Chicago to enter Harvard Law School. He became the first African American president of the Harvard Law Review. He graduated magna cum laude in 1991. He returned to Chicago where he began teaching at the University of Chicago Law School and attained a position at the civil rights law firm Miner, Barnhill & Galland.

In 1996, Obama won an Illinois State Senate seat. During his time in the Illinois Senate, Obama was instrumental in his work with both Democrats and Republicans toward the passage of legislation on ethics and health care reform. In addition, he was also responsible for legislation aimed at death penalty reform and the obligatory videotaping of homicide interrogations.

After four years in the State Senate, Obama ran an unsuccessful campaign in the primary election for a U.S. House of Representatives seat against incumbent Bobby Rush.

On July 27, 2004, Obama, a candidate for the U.S. Senate, was the keynote speaker at the Democratic National Convention. While his speech urged the nation to elect John Kerry for President, it was Obama's story about his family, his political views, and his hope for a better future for America that spurred him into national prominence. With the momentum behind him, Obama won the Illinois U.S. Senate seat by a landslide over his Republican rival Alan Keyes.

In February 2007, Obama announced his candidacy for the 2008 Democratic presidential nominee. He has run a campaign that has focused on bringing change to Washington and uniting the country. He has gained the support and endorsements of Oprah Winfrey, Toni Morrison, Ted Kennedy, Caroline Kennedy, and Maria Shriver.

He has been in a heated race against former first lady and U.S. Senator Hillary Rodham Clinton. Democratic presidential hopeful, John Edwards, withdrew from the race on January 30, 2008, one day after he placed third in a non-binding primary election in Florida. After winning a string of primary elections, Obama's campaign faced heated questions over his association with Trinity's pastor Rev. Wright. Some of Wright's sermons sparked controversy and questions over Obama's beliefs about America and racial relations. Obama addressed these concerns, but the controversy continued and was renewed once again when guest speaker Rev. Michael Pfleger made controversial remarks while speaking at Trinity. On May 31, 2008, Obama publically announced that he had withdrawn his membership from the church.

On June 3, 2008, Obama won enough delegates to clinch the Democratic presidential nomination. He is the first person of black heritage to become the presidential nominee of a major political party.

Obama is the author of three books: *Dreams from My Father* (1995), *The Audacity of Hope* (2006), and *It Takes a Nation: How Strangers Became Family in the Wake of Hurricane Katrina* (2006).

Obama has been married to his wife, Michelle, since 1992. They have two daughters, Malia and Sasha, and live in Kenwood, a Chicago community.

COLIN POWELL
(1937 – Present)

Occupation: military official, general, secretary of state

Colin Powell was born in New York City on April 5, 1937. He was raised in the South Bronx by his parents who were immigrants from Jamaica.

After attending public schools, Powell attended the City College of New York, and received his bachelor's degree in geology in 1958. While in college, he participated in the ROTC program. Upon graduation, the Army appointed him as a second lieutenant.

In 1962, Powell served as a military advisor in Vietnam. Six years later, the army appointed him as battalion executive officer and division operations officer in Vietnam. He returned to the United States in 1969, and earned his MBA from George Washington University in 1971.

114

In 1972, Powell served as the assistant to the deputy director of the Office of Management and Budget. Thereafter, he served in several government positions. From 1983 to 1986, he served as the senior military assistant to the Secretary of Defense. In 1987, he was appointed as the Assistant to the President for National Security Affairs. He served in this position until 1989, when he was appointed as the 12th Chairman of the Joint Chiefs of Staff. In this position, he oversaw Operation Desert Storm of the Persian Gulf War.

In 1993, Powell retired from military service. During his career, he received numerous medals. They include the Purple Heart and Bronze Star (1963), Soldiers Medal and the Secretary's Award (1988), and the Ronald Reagan Freedom Award (1988). After retirement, Powell published his autobiography, *My American Journey* (1995). As Powell traveled around the country to promote his book, there was speculation as to whether he would run for President in 1996; he declined to run. Instead, Powell embarked upon a public speaking career that led him throughout the United States and abroad.

In 1997, Powell began serving as chairman of America's Promise – The Alliance for Youth, a non-profit organization promoting character development and competence of young people. He served as chairman until President George W. Bush nominated him the Secretary of State on December 16, 2000. On January 20, 2001, he was sworn in. In November 2004, Powell resigned after President Bush won reelection.

MUHAMMAD ALI
(January 17, 1942 – present)

Occupation: boxer

Muhammad Ali was born Cassius Marcellus Clay, Jr. to Cassius Marcellus Clay, Sr. and Odessa (Grady) Clay on January 17, 1942 in Louisville, Kentucky. Clay's father worked painting billboards and signs, and his mother worked as a domestic. Clay began boxing at the age of twelve, under the direction of Joe Martin. He began fighting in the amateur ranks. In the 1960 Olympic Games in Rome, he won a gold medal in the 175-pound division.

After the Olympics, Clay emerged in the professional league under the sponsorship of the Louisville Sponsoring Group. In October 1960, in his first professional heavyweight fight against Tunney Hunsaker, he won. After winning his next eighteen fights, fifteen by knockout, Clay was scheduled to fight the heavyweight champion Sonny Liston on February 25, 1964 in Miami Beach, Florida.

Clay was considered the underdog to Liston who had knocked out his last three challengers in the first round. Before the fight, as Clay was known to do, he verbally attacked Liston and boasted that he would win. To the shock of the boxing world, Clay's prediction came true. He defeated Liston.

Two days after the fight, Clay announced that he was converting to the Nation of Islam. On March 6, 1964, he changed his name to Muhammad Ali, which was the name given to him by Elijah Muhammad. This was so contro-versial that during the 1960s, the *New York Times* and several other papers refused to acknowledge his new name when writing about him.

Ali fought a rematch with Liston on May 25, 1965. Ali knocked out Liston in the first round. Over the next two years, Ali defended his title and won against Floyd Patterson, George Chuvalo, Henry Cooper, Brian London, Karl Mildenberger, Cleveland Williams, Ernie Terrell, and Zora Folley.

On April 28, 1967, Ali made another controversial decision. When drafted in the U.S. Army during the war in Vietnam, he refused to go. For Ali, his opposition stemmed from more than just his belief that the war was immoral. He believed that since blacks did not experience equality at home, for them to serve in the war was a perversion of justice.

Initially, Ali was granted conscientious objector status, but after he stated that he was not against all wars and would participate in an Islamic holy war, he no longer qualified. He was fined ten thousand dollars, sentenced to five years in prison, and his heavyweight title and license to box was taken away. Four years later, his conviction was overturned by the U.S. Supreme court because of procedural grounds.

Ali returned to professional boxing in October 1970. Although his skills had eroded and he was less agile than before, he was victorious over Jerry Quarry and Oscar Bonavena. The challenge came when he fought Joe Frazier in the match called the "Fight of the Century". On March 8, 1971, Ali lost to Frazier. In a second match with Frazier, he won.

After years of working his way closer to the heavyweight title, on October 30, 1974, Ali fought heavyweight champion, George Foreman. The fight took place in Kinshasa, Zaire (now called the Democratic Republic of the Congo), and it was referred to as the "Rumble in the Jungle". Ali was the favorite for the people of Zaire, and Foreman was considered the American. In the eighth round, Ali knocked out Foreman. He regained the heavyweight title for a second time.

Before retirement, Ali had a few other notable fights. He fought a third match against Frazier. Called the "Thrilla in Manila", the fight took place on October 1, 1975 in Manila, Philippines. Ali celebrated another victory over Frazier. On February 15, 1978, he lost his title to Olympic gold medalist, Leon Spinks. Less than a year later, he defeated Spinks, and for the third time he held the heavyweight title.

Ali retired in 1979, but returned to the ring in 1980 to fight Larry Holmes. His skills had substantially diminished and he suffered the worst loss of his career. He returned for his last fight in 1981 against Trevor Berbick. While not as brutal as his prior fight, he lost again.

In the late 1980s, Ali began suffering from Parkinson's disease. Despite this hurdle, Ali remained active. He was the spokesperson for Operation USA in Rwanda in 1996, he formed the Muhammad Ali Community and Economic Development Corporation in Chicago, Illinois, and in 1996 he lit the opening flame at the Olympic Games in Atlanta.

118

DENZEL WASHINGTON
(December 28, 1954 – Present)

Occupation: actor, director

Denzel Washington was born in Mount Vernon, New York on December 28, 1954. He was the second of three children born to a preacher father, and a mother who worked as a hairdresser. Washington spent some time in a boarding school when he was fourteen years old, but more significant in his young life was the time he spent at the local Boys and Girls Club. It was Washington's involvement in the club that he attributes to keeping him off the street and out of trouble.

From high school, Washington went on to attend Fordham University. It was there that his acting abilities became apparent. He appeared in the student production of *The Emperor Jones*, but it was his ability to win the lead part in the school's production of *Othello* that really showed his talent. In 1977, he graduated from Fordham with a bachelor's degree in journalism.

By this time, Washington was certain that he wanted to pursue acting. He moved to San Francisco, where he enrolled in the American Conservatory Theatre. Shortly thereafter, he secured a role as Wilma Rudolph's boyfriend in the television production of *Wilma* (1977). Washington went on to appear as Private Peterson in *A Soldier's Play*. In 1982, Washington's big break came when he was cast as Dr. Philip Chandler in the popular television series *St. Elsewhere*.

By the time the show ended in 1988, Washington was ready to leave the television set behind and take on movie roles. In 1987, his performance in *Cry Freedom* earned him an Academy Award nomination for best supporting actor. But it was his portrayal of Private Trip in *Glory* (1989) that won him an Oscar for best supporting actor.

In 1990, Washington teamed up with the up-and-coming director Spike Lee for the film *Mo' Better Blues*. He played Bleek Gilliam, a jazz trumpeter who faced challenges in his personal relationships and his career. Two years later, Washington reunited with Spike Lee for the film *Malcolm X*. Once again, Washington was nominated for an Oscar, but this time it was for best actor.

In 1999, Washington was nominated for best actor for his role as Rubin "Hurricane" Carter in *The Hurricane*. However, it was his role as Alonzo Harris, a corrupt L.A.P.D. narcotics officer in the movie *Training Day* (2001), that earned him an Oscar for best actor. In 2007, Washington was nominated for a Golden Globe for best actor for his portrayal of Frank Lucas in *American Gangster*.

Besides acting, Washington has become a director. His directorial debut occurred in 2002 with the release of Antwone Fisher. Besides directing the film, Washington co-starred as Dr. Jerome Davenport, the psychiatrist charged with treating Fisher. In 2007, Washington once again took on the role as director and actor in the film *The Great Debaters*. The film has been nominated for best picture by the Golden Globe.

Washington is married to Pauletta Pearson, whom he met on the set while filming *Wilma*. They have four children together and live in Los Angeles, California.

Besides acting and directing, Washington is a committed proponent and supporter of the Boys and Girls Clubs of America, and he supports other charities including the AIDS hospice, the Gathering Place, and the Nelson Mandela Children's Fund.

BENJAMIN BANNEKER
(November 9, 1731 – October 25, 1806)

Occupation: inventor, astronomer

Unlike many African Americans at the time, Benjamin Banneker was not born into slavery. The maternal side of his family determined this fate. His grandmother, Mary Walsh, was a white Englishwoman who was sentenced to seven years of indentured servitude in America for stealing milk. After her servitude ended, she bought some land and two African slaves. She married one of them. His name was Bannaky, and they had many children, one of whom was named Mary. Like her mother, when Mary married, she bought a slave and married him. Mary and Robert had several children, including Benjamin Banneker. Banneker was born on November 9, 1731, just outside of Baltimore, Maryland.

Benjamin Banneker made his mark on history with his contributions to astronomy, science, and math. He became known for building the first wooden clock, his almanacs, and for his part in building the capital city. Most notable about his accomplishments was that, despite racial constraints and little formal education, he was a self-taught man. By the end of his life, his achievements were well known around the world.

RICHARD ALLEN
(February 14, 1760 – March 26, 1831)

Occupation: Bishop

Richard Allen was born a slave in Philadelphia, Pennsylvania to the estate of a prominent lawyer. Not long after, Allen and his family were sold to Stokeley Sturgis, a Delaware planter. While a slave, Allen became a Methodist, and began preaching to the unconverted, including to his owner. Eventually Sturgis was influenced by the Methodists teaching that slave ownership was wrong, and thus, he allowed Allen to buy his freedom.

As a free man, Allen traveled throughout South Carolina, New York, Maryland, Delaware, and Pennsylvania, working odd jobs to support himself, while at the same time, preaching in Methodist churches. While in Philadelphia, he accepted a position as the Methodist preacher for the black parishioners at St. George's Methodist Church.

In 1787, Allen joined with Absalom Jones to create the Free African Society, a non-denominational aid society. When the organization built a church and offered Allen the position of pastor of the St. Thomas African Episcopal Church, he rejected it and formed his own church for black Methodist parishioners; in 1794, Allen founded Bethel African Methodist Church. Although his church enjoyed constant growth, over time the Methodist organization became more controlling over black congregations. In response, in 1816, several black Methodist churches came together to form the African Methodist Episcopal Church, the first black denomination. Allen served as the Church's first bishop until his death in 1831.

LOUIS ARMSTRONG
(August 4, 1901 – July 6, 1971)

Occupation: jazz musician, singer

Also known as: Satchmo

Louis Armstrong was born in New Orleans on August 4, 1901, to an unmarried fifteen-year-old mother. He and his mother lived in the poorest and most crime-ridden neighborhood known as "The Battlefield". At the age of twelve, Armstrong was arrested for delinquency and sent to the Colored Waif's Home. While there, he joined the brass band and played the cornet.

From the beginning, it was apparent that Armstrong was a natural. After his release, he continued to play the cornet. He was too young to join the cabaret, so he played in the streets. Finally, at sixteen, he received the opportunity from Edward "Kid" Ory to sit-in for his absent cornet player Joseph "King" Oliver. After this experience, Armstrong received the opportunity to play in Fate Marable's Kentucky Jazz Band, which performed on a Mississippi riverboat.

In 1922, Armstrong moved to Chicago to play second cornet in Oliver's band. The pianist, Lil Hardin, a Fisk University graduate, immediately liked Armstrong. She convinced him to leave Oliver's band, taught him how to act and dress, and then married him. Armstrong and Hardin moved to New

York City where he joined the Fletcher Henderson Orchestra.

In 1925, he returned to Chicago where he and other musicians recorded the Hot Five and Hot Seven recordings. It was on these recordings that jazz history was changed. Armstrong introduced the jazz soloist as the focal point and scat singing. The recordings featured Armstrong playing the trumpet in such hits as "Muggles", "Potato Head Blues", "Hotter than Hot", and "Wild Man Blues".

While the Hot Five and Hot Seven recordings garnered attention, it was not until 1929 that Armstrong became famous. His performance of "Ain't Misbehavin" in the Broadway show *Hot Chocolates* pushed his career to new heights. In the 1930s and 1940s, Armstrong had parts in over fifty films, a radio show, and he toured America and Europe as a solo trumpet player accompanied by big bands. His recordings not only featured him playing the trumpet, but also him singing the lyrics in a husky voice that became his recognizable trademark. Such works included, "Body and Soul", "Star Dust", "Hobo", and "You Can't Ride This Train".

Armstrong's career continued into the 1960s with film appearances, popular hits, and a world tour with All-Stars sextets. His popular hits included "Hello, Dolly", "Blueberry Hill", and "Mack the Knife". His last film appearance was in *Hello, Dolly!* in 1969. On July 6, 1971, Armstrong died of heart failure.

ARTHUR ASHE
(July 10, 1943 – February 6, 1993)

Occupation: tennis player

Arthur Ashe was born in Richmond, Virginia on July 10, 1943. When he was just seven years old, he began playing tennis. Ashe, like Althea Gibson, was coached by Walter Johnson. By the time he was eighteen, he had become good enough to receive a tennis scholarship to UCLA.

While at UCLA, Ashe became a nationally recognized tennis player. In 1963, he was selected for the U.S. Davis Cup team, and he became the first African American team member. In 1965, Ashe won singles and doubles titles in the national collegiate championship. Ashe's other victories included the U.S. Open (1968), the Australian Open (1970), and Wimbledon (1975).

Ashe was instrumental in the formation of the Association of Tennis Professionals (ATP). The ATP changed how tennis players earned money. At the time, players received very little in prize money for playing in tournaments. The ATP changed that by providing more substantial prize money to tournament competitors.

In addition to his success as a tennis player, Ashe also spoke out against injustice. When South Africa denied his visa for the South African Open, Ashe garnered public support. As a result, on March 23, 1970, South Africa was excluded from the Davis Cup competition.

In 1980, Ashe retired from tennis. Five years later, he was elected into the Tennis Hall of Fame. Ashe also found success outside of tennis. In 1988, his three-volume book, *A Hard Road to Glory*, was published. *Daddy and Me* and *Days of Grace* followed in 1993.

In 1992, Ashe publicly announced that he had contracted the HIV virus from a blood transfusion during heart surgery in 1983. He died on February 6, 1993.

GEORGE WASHINGTON CARVER
(1864? – January 5, 1943)

Occupation: inventor, agricultural chemist

Patents: U.S. 1,522,176 Cosmetics and Producing the Same. January 6, 1925. George W. Carver. Tuskegee, Alabama.

U.S. 1,541,478 Paint and Stain and Producing the Same June 9, 1925. George W. Carver. Tuskegee, Alabama.

U.S. 1,632,365 Producing Paints and Stains. June 14, 1927. George W. Carver. Tuskegee, Alabama.

Some Inventions by George W. Carver: Adhesives, Axle Grease, Bleach, Buttermilk, Cheese, Chili Sauce, Cream, Creosote, Dyes, Flour, Fuel Briquettes, Ink, Instant Coffee, Insulating Board, Linoleum, Mayonnaise, Meal, Meat Tenderizer, Metal Polish, Milk Flakes, Mucilage, Paper, Rubbing Oils, Salve, Soil Conditioner, Shampoo, Shoe Polish, Shaving Cream, Sugar, Synthetic Marble, Synthetic Rubber, Talcum Powder, Vanishing Cream, Wood Stains, Wood Filler, and Worcestershire Sauce.

George Washington Carver was born a slave in Diamond Grove, Missouri. When he was an infant, Confederate raiders kidnapped him and his mother. When the Civil War ended, Carver's master, Moses Carver, was able to locate him and bring him back to Missouri. However, he was unable to find his mother. Moses Carver and his wife raised Carver.

Carver began his education at a school in Newton County, Missouri. At the same time, he moved from the Carver family home and began working as a farm hand. He went on to attend Minneapolis High School in Kansas and Simpson College. Carver later transferred to Iowa Agricultural College (now Iowa State University). In 1894, he received his B.S. in agricultural science, and three years later, he received his M.S. in agriculture. After graduating, Carver took a faculty position at Iowa College.

Carver's time at Iowa College, however, was short lived. When Booker T. Washington offered him a position at the newly opened Tuskegee Normal and Industrial Institute in 1897, Carver readily accepted. While at Tuskegee, Carver developed a crop rotation method which alternated cotton crops with soil enriching crops such as peanuts, sweet potato, and pecans. Carver also developed over 300 uses for peanuts and numerous uses for sweet potatoes and pecans.

Despite Carver's many innovations, he held only three patents for his inventions of soybean-based paints and stains. According to Carver, he felt strongly that he should not financially benefit from his inventions. Instead, he believed that his discoveries should be freely shared.

In 1923, he was awarded the Spingarn Medal by the National Association for the Advancement of Colored People (NAACP). In 1938, he gave his life savings of $30,000 to the George Washington Carver Foundation.

After his death on January 5, 1943, a national monument was dedicated to his memory on July 14, 1943.

FREDRICK DOUGLASS
(February 1818 – February 20, 1895)

Born a slave, yet determined to be free, Frederick Douglass escaped from slavery and became one of the most influential figures of the 19th century. He became a powerful speaker in the anti-slavery circuit, an author, an advocate for women's rights, and held several government positions after the Civil War.

In 1832, after Douglass Aaron Anthony died, he went to live with Thomas Auld on the Lloyd Plantation. In 1834, his new master hired him out to Edward Covey, a slave breaker who was known for whipping and working slaves hard. He endured many whippings until the day that he fought back and prevailed. This event gave Douglass spirit again. In 1836, he made an unsuccessful attempt to escape. He was soon sent back to Baltimore.

His second attempt was successful. Equipped with the identification papers of a sailor friend, he dressed as a sailor and traveled to New York City by train and steamboat. On September 3, 1838, he escaped from slavery. Shortly after his arrival, he married Anna Murray, a free black woman he had met in Baltimore. They settled in New Bedford, Massachusetts. During their marriage, they had five children together.

In 1841, Douglass began his life as a public figure and abolitionist. After hearing William Lloyd Garrison's anti-slavery speech, Douglass was inspired to tell his story. He spoke at the Massachusetts Anti-Slavery Society annual convention about his experience as a slave. His speech was powerful and eloquent. He was encouraged by Garrison, who became his mentor, to continue speaking.

In 1845, he wrote about his life as a slave in the *Narrative of the Life of Frederick Douglass, An American Slave*. After its publication, he traveled to England, Scotland, and Ireland where he continued speaking against slavery. Upon his return to the United States in 1847, he moved to New York and published the weekly paper called the *North Star*.

During the Civil War, he was active in recruiting black soldiers for the Union Army. Douglass also became an advocate of women's rights. Later in his life, he served the government in several positions. From 1877 to 1881, he was the U.S. Marshall of the District of Columbia, from 1881 to 1886 he served as the recorder of deeds for the District of Columbia, and from 1889 to 1891 he was the minister to Haiti.

After Douglass' wife died in 1882, he married his former secretary, Helen Pitts, in 1884. On February 20, 1895, after speaking at the National Council of Women, he died of heart failure at his home, Cedar Hill, in Anacostia, Washington, D.C.

CHARLES DREW
(June 3, 1904 – April 1, 1950)

In 1938, Drew received a two-year Rockefeller Fellowship to study blood at Columbia University Presbyterian Hospital in New York. While at Columbia, Drew made a remarkable discovery. At the time, stored blood only lasted seven days;

Drew discovered that by using plasma, blood without the cells, it could be stored longer.

This was both a revolutionary discovery and a timely one. England was entering into World War II, and blood was essential to saving the lives of injured soldiers. In 1940, Drew's discovery led to his recruitment to take charge of collecting, organizing, and sending blood plasma to England. One year later, when his position ended, he became the director of the American Red Cross' program to collect blood.

As he had done for the English program, he was in charge of all aspects of blood collection. In the midst of his work for the American Red Cross, the military made a controversial decision. It ordered the segregation of blood from African American donators. Drew and other medical professionals argued, albeit without success, that there was no difference between white and African American blood. Nevertheless, segregated blood became military policy.

In May 1941, Drew made the hard decision to resign from his position as the director of the American Red Cross. Some scholars have asserted that he left in protest of the segregated blood issue. However, according to scholar Louis Haber, in an interview with Drew's widow, she stated that his reason for leaving was to return to his real passion, the practice of surgery. Drew left the Red Cross and returned to Howard University and to the resident training program in surgery at the Freedmen's Hospital.

At the time, Drew was one of the few African American physicians who were held in such high regard in the medical community. It is not hard to see why. In addition to his discovery of plasma use, he also was the first African

130

American to earn a Doctor of Science degree (1940), and he became the first black surgeon examiner of the American Board of Surgery (1942). For his plasma work, he received the NAACP Spingarn Medal in 1944.

Unfortunately, Charles Drew died young. On April 1, 1950, while driving three of his students to a medical meeting at Tuskegee Institute in Alabama, Drew fell asleep at the wheel. His passengers only suffered injuries, but Drew did not survive.

WILLIAM EDWARD BURGHARDT DU BOIS
(February 23, 1868 – August 27, 1963)

Considered one of the most influential black intellectuals of the 20th century, W.E.B. Du Bois encouraged intellectual development, economic independence, and helped found the NAACP. In his early career, he experienced great success, but as his views moved toward Black Nationalism and socialism, support for his ideas waned. By the end of his life, he had renounced his United States citizenship and moved to Ghana.

In 1897, he joined the faculty at Atlanta University. In 1903, his collection of essays was published in his most famous work, *The Souls of Black Folk*. In it he argued the "the color line" was the central problem of the 20th century. He also rejected Booker T. Washington's argument for accommodation and for the promotion of training blacks to work in trades. While Washington promoted industrial training, Du Bois focused on intellectual advancement.

In 1905, Du Bois and William Monroe Trotter, editor of the *Boston Guardian*, formed the Niagara Movement. The organization sought to obtain civil and political rights for blacks and challenged Booker T. Washington's ideas. It existed for only a short time.

Despite the failing of the Niagara Movement, in 1909 Du Bois helped found the interracial organization, the NAACP. Du Bois served as the director of research and was the editor of its magazine *The Crisis*.

In addition to his work for the NAACP, Du Bois also had an interest in Black Nationalism and socialism. As an advocate of Pan-Africanism, he organized the first Pan-African Conference in 1900 and another in 1919. Du Bois encouraged the intellectual development of blacks and promoted the idea of a group economy as a way to fight discrimination and poverty. In 1912, he joined the Socialist party for a brief time.

In 1920, he published the controversial book *Darkwater: Voices from Within the Veil*. As his views changed, so did his vision on the direction that the NAACP should take. Du Bois believed the organization should focus on black economic development as opposed to fighting discrimination. In 1934, he resigned as editor of *The Crisis*.

He returned to Atlanta University where he began teaching again. Also, during this time, he published several books, including *Black Reconstruction* (1933), *Dusk of Dawn: An Essay Toward an Autobiography of a Race Concept* (1940), and *Color and Democracy, Colonies and Peace* (1945). In 1939, he also founded *Phylon*, a somewhat radical journal that explored racial issues. In 1944, he was forced to resign from Atlanta University. He returned to the NAACP in 1944 where he served in a research position. After renewed disagreement with the NAACP, he was dismissed in 1948.

In 1951, Du Bois and four others were indicted under the Foreign Agents Registration Act and charged with not registering as agents of a foreign government. Du Bois and the others were acquitted. However, the government and colleagues shunned him because of his socialist leaning, and he remained disconnected from the civil rights movement.

In 1961, he moved to Ghana where he began to work on the *Encyclopedia Africana*, and he also became a citizen of Ghana. He died in 1963 before he could finish his encyclopedia.

MEDGAR EVERS
(July 2, 1925 – June 12, 1963)

In addition to working, Evers dedicated his time to working on behalf of the National Association for the Advancement of Colored People (NAACP). When the United States Supreme Court made its ruling in Brown v. Board of Education (1954) to end segregation in public schools, Evers decided to test the decision by applying to the University of Mississippi Law School. His attempt was unsuccessful.

Shortly thereafter, Evers moved to Jackson, Mississippi where he became the first Mississippi field secretary for the NAACP. His job involved recruiting members, voter registration drives, economic boycotts, and political sit-ins.

Because of Evers' new position, he soon became the target of violent threats. A threat was soon carried out in May 1963 when his home was firebombed. Neither Evers nor his family was hurt. However, the second threat carried out was fatal. On June 12, 1963, Evers was shot in the back in the driveway of his home. He died within an hour at a local hospital.

MARCUS GARVEY
(August 17, 1887 – June 10, 1940)

Occupation: social activist

Also Known As: Black Moses

Jamaican born nationalist leader Marcus Garvey quickly rose in popularity during the World War I era. As quickly as his rise in prominence, however, without the support of his ideology from other black leaders, his popularity was brief.

Marcus Garvey was born in Jamaica on August 17, 1887. He attended school until he was fourteen. In 1910, he traveled to Central America. He served as the editor for the daily newspaper, *La Nacion*, while living in Colon, Panama. In 1912, he returned to Jamaica, but soon left for London to attend Birbeck College.

When he returned to Jamaica in 1914, Garvey and Amy Ashwood co-founded the Universal Negro Improvement and Conservation Association and African Communities League. The association became known as the Universal Negro Improvement Association (UNIA). Through this organization, Garvey sought to organize blacks throughout the world and create societies in Africa. He also wanted to establish an independent black economy based on capitalism.

In Jamaica, the UNIA failed to attract a substantial following, so Garvey came to New York in 1916. He established branches of the UNIA throughout the northern cities. He also began publishing his newspaper, *Negro World*. His publication incited considerable attention. In Belize and other countries, it was considered seditious and was confiscated.

By 1919, his following had reached 2,000,000. That same year, he established the shipping company, the Black Star Line, and the Negro Factories Corporation. He also opened a chain of restaurants, grocery stores, laundries, a hotel, and a printing press.

The U.S. government began to notice Garvey's activities. In 1919, the Bureau of Investigation started to monitor his actions. With the intent to eventually deport him, the bureau began to gather evidence of his actions that related to the Black Star Line.

During his peak in popularity, in 1920, he presided over the UNIA's first international convention. The convention included delegates from 25 countries. Among the actions taken was the adoption of *The Declaration of Rights of the Negro People of the World* and the election of Garvey as the Provisional President of Africa.

Despite his following, Garvey's ideology of racial purity and separatism failed to gain the support of black leaders such as W.E.B. Du Bois. In addition, in 1922, the Black Star Line was dissolved. Garvey's other businesses also failed. Garvey received an additional blow when he was indicted for mail fraud for the sale of Black Star Line stock. In 1923, he was convicted and sentenced to five years in prison. In 1925, he began serving his prison sentence. After President Calvin Coolidge commuted his sentence in 1927, he was deported to Jamaica. He died in obscurity in London, England in 1940.

LANGSTON HUGHES
(February 1, 1902 – May 22, 1967)

Occupation: writer, poet

Harlem Renaissance writer and poet, Langston Hughes, was one of the more notable writers during this time. Known for his portrayal of black life in his work, Hughes' success was partly due to his ability to effectively capture the essence of the black experience.

Many of Hughes' writings reflected his outlook on the world. For instance, during the depression, his work mirrored his socialist attitude, and during World War II, some of his literature was patriotic in its tone. He also explored segregation, the life of ordinary blacks, and black culture. It was not uncommon for Hughes' inspiration to come while sitting in jazz clubs listening music; a good deal of his work was influenced by jazz.

Hughes wrote poetry, short stories, novels, plays, children's books, and magazine articles. His work includes *The Dream Keeper* (1932), *The Big Sea* (1940), *Shakespeare in Harlem* (1942), *Fields of Wonder* (1947), *The Poetry of the Negro* (1949), *Montage of a Dream Deferred* (1951), *I Wonder as I Wander* (1956), *Tambourines to Glory* (1958), and *The Book of Negro Folklore* (1958).

Hughes died of cancer on May 22, 1967. His home, located at 20 East 127th Street in Harlem, was declared a landmark by the New York City Preservation Commission.

136

MARTIN LURTHER KING JR.
(January 15, 1929 – April 4, 1968)

Intelligent, dedicated, charismatic, and religious, Martin Luther King Jr. had what it took to inspire the conscience of the American public. He appealed to the moral sense of Americans, and after years of leading civil rights activists in nonviolent protest and direct action, his leadership helped to desegregate the South.

In 1954, King became the pastor of Dexter Avenue Baptist Church in Montgomery, Alabama. Shortly thereafter, on December 1, 1955, Rosa Parks was arrested after she refused to give up her seat to a white rider on a Montgomery city bus. Based on Parks decision to contest the arrest, the Montgomery Improvement Association was founded in order to organize the boycott of city buses. The members of the association elected King as president.

Nonviolent resistance slowly began to emerge as the defining force in the protest. During the boycott, King received numerous threats, and his home was bombed. King and his family were not harmed, but this led to his concrete belief in the effectiveness of nonviolent resistance. After more than a year, the boycott ended when the United States Supreme Court affirmed the District Court order to desegregate the city buses.

After successfully navigating the bus boycott, King had emerged as a national figure. King and other ministers founded the Southern Christian Leadership Conference (SCLC), which served to organize civil rights protest movements throughout the South.

--------------------A Black Man's Worth!--------------------

In 1959, King furthered his knowledge of Gandhi's nonviolent philosophy when he visited India. Upon his return, he moved to Atlanta, Georgia to co-pastor with his father at Ebenezer Baptist Church. While a co-pastor, King also stayed involved with the SCLC.

In October 1960, King participated in the student sit-in movement. He was arrested and sentenced to serve time in prison. His sentence received nationwide media attention. After President Dwight Eisenhower decided not to intervene, presidential candidate John F. Kennedy got involved, and King was released.

King continued to participate in nonviolent protest. By 1963, however, King felt that civil rights progress was stagnant. King, A. Philip Randolph, Bayard Rustin, and several other civil rights leaders organized the March on Washington for Jobs and Freedom. At the march, on August 28, 1963, King gave his famous "I Have a Dream" speech. More than 250,000 blacks and whites who had gathered at the Lincoln Memorial witnessed this memorable speech.

In 1963, King became *Time* magazine's "Man of the Year." One year later, he received the Noble Peace Prize. This was also an important year for the civil rights movement. As the movement had garnered widespread support, the Civil Rights Act of 1964 was passed.

After 1965, disenfranchisement with King surfaced among African Americans who became impatient with his method of nonviolent resistance. During the 1965 Selma, Alabama march for voting rights, opposition became more prevalent when the marchers, who were led by King, marched across the Edmund Pettus Bridge, but stopped when confronted by a barricade of state troopers. King and the marchers kneeled, prayed, and then turned around.

Radical African Americans believed that King should have handled the situation differently. Furthermore, as the black power movement became stronger and as Malcolm X's message of Black Nationalism became more accepted by Northern urban blacks, King increasingly became a controversial figure.

Despite the growing dissatisfaction with King's tactics, he expanded his focus to include opposition to the Vietnam War. However, King's disagreement with the war led to strained relations with the Lyndon B. Johnson administration.

King also began focusing on the poor of all races. In the spring of 1968, in the midst of planning the Poor People's March on Washington, King left for Memphis, Tennessee to lead a strike of city sanitation workers. It was there that he delivered his last speech, "I've Been to the Mountaintop."

The next day, on April 4, 1968, while standing on the balcony of his motel, he was shot. He was 39 years old. A few months later, on June 8, 1968, James Earl Ray was arrested in London, England. Ray pled guilty and was sentenced to ninety-nine years in prison.

THURGOOD MARSHALL
(July 2, 1908 – January 24, 1993)

U.S. Supreme Court Justice, attorney

Thurgood Marshall is most known for serving as the first black United States Supreme Court Justice, but prior to his career on the bench, he successfully argued civil rights cases on behalf of the National Association for the Advancement of Colored People (NAACP). In 1936, Marshall began working for the NAACP, and later became the director of NAACP's Legal Defense and Education Fund.

Marshall argued 32 cases before the U.S. Supreme Court and won 29 of them. These cases included *Smith v. Allwright* (1944), *Morgan v. Virginia* (1946), *Shelley v. Kramer* (1948), and *Sweatt v. Painter* (1950). Marshall also argued and won the landmark case Brown v. Board of Education (1954), which made segregation in public schools unconstitutional.

In 1961, Marshall's success as an attorney was duly noted when President John F. Kennedy nominated him to the United States Court of Appeals for the Second Circuit. Marshall's nomination was met with opposition, but months later, he was finally confirmed by the Senate. In July 1965, President Lyndon Johnson appointed Marshall as the U.S. Solicitor General. Shortly thereafter, in 1967, President Johnson nominated him to the U.S. Supreme Court.

As a Supreme Court Justice, Marshall was a strong advocate for civil rights and was steadfast in his goal to end discrimination.

Marshall retired from the court in 1991. He died on January 24, 1993.

ELIJAH MCCOY
(May 2, 1844 – October 10, 1929)

Occupation: mechanical engineer, inventor

Elijah McCoy was born on May 2, 1844, in Colchester, Ontario in Canada. His parents were fugitive Kentucky slaves who escaped slave owners through the Underground Railroad. His family later moved back to the United States and settled west of Ypsilanti, Michigan. As a youth, McCoy had an interest in machinery and other mechanical things. Thus, after attending grammar school, he left for Edinburgh, Scotland for an apprenticeship in mechanical engineering.

After completing his apprenticeship, McCoy returned to the United States with training as a mechanical engineer. He searched for a job as an engineer, but encountered racial prejudice. Unable to obtain an engineering job, he instead settled on a job as a fireman for the Michigan Central Railroad, where he oiled the engines.

While this was not a job as a mechanical engineer, it did inspire his first invention. McCoy became interested in the process of the lubrication of machines. He observed that in order to oil the train engines, the trains were stopped, and an oilman oiled the moving parts. Because lubrication was essential and time consuming, McCoy began to explore ways to make the process of oiling more efficient.

After tinkering around in his machine shop, McCoy created a device called the "lubricating cup". On July 12, 1872,

McCoy patented his first invention, an automatic lubricator. This device allowed machines to continue to operate as oil continuously flowed to the gears and the moving parts. McCoy's invention revolutionized the machine industry.

From thereafter, McCoy began inventing other mechanisms. In 1892, McCoy invented devices to lubricate railroad locomotives. In the 1920s, McCoy applied his lubricating system to airbrakes used on locomotives and other vehicles using air brakes. Almost all of McCoy's patents related to automatic lubrication, with the exception of a patent for an ironing table and a lawn sprinkler. Upon his death on October 10, 1929, McCoy had patented over fifty inventions.

GARRETT MORGAN
(March 4, 1877 – July 27, 1963)

Inventor Garrett Morgan started his career out as a sewing machine adjuster, but his creativity and intelligence led him on a new path. Among his numerous ideas, Morgan invented the gas mask and the traffic signal, two indispensable inventions that have both saved lives and made life safer. In 1909, he pursued several ventures. He opened a tailoring shop, which employed 32 workers, and he created his first invention. While experimenting with chemicals for a solution to prevent thread from scorching when sewing wool material, Morgan came across a solution to straightening curly hair. The chemical solution that he used to experiment with had straightened the fuzz on the cloth used to wipe his hands.

This gave him an idea. First, he experimented with the chemical on his neighbor's dog, and then on himself. Both times, he was able to straighten hair. Morgan patented the solution, and created the product G.A. Morgan Hair Refining Cream.

In 1912, Morgan made another invention. He created the Safety Hood, also known as the gas mask. He patented it in 1914, naming it a Breathing Device. The device had a hood that was attached to a long tube with an opening for air, and a second tube with a valve that exhaled air. At the Second International Exposition of Safety and Sanitation in New York City, Morgan received first prize for his invention. Morgan's invention was put to the test on July 24, 1916, when there was an explosion in a Cleveland Water Works tunnel. Thirty-two men were trapped in the smoke and gas filled tunnel. Morgan and his brother Frank entered the tunnel wearing Safety Hoods. They were able to carry out the men, but not all survived. This incident gave Morgan and his invention substantial notoriety.

In 1923, Morgan had another idea. He noticed that the combination of cars and horse drawn carriages on the road created confusion and accidents. As a result, he invented a traffic light signal. On November 20, 1923, Morgan patented his traffic signal in the U.S., and later patented it in England and Canada. He eventually sold the rights to the General Electric Corporation for $40,000.

Besides being an inventor, Morgan was active in his community. He created the black newspaper the *Cleveland Call*, which later became known as the *Call & Post*. In 1914, he began serving as the treasurer of the Cleveland Association of Colored Men. When it later merged with the NAACP, he became a member. Lastly, in an effort to represent black constituents, Morgan made an unsuccessful run for the Cleveland City Council.

In 1943, Morgan contracted glaucoma and lost 90 percent of his eyesight. He died on July 27, 1963.

JESSE OWENS
(September 12, 1913 – March 31, 1980)

Occupation: track and field athlete, Olympic medalist

Frail and often sickly as a child, who would have guessed that Jesse Owens would go on to achieve the status of an Olympic medalist. With Hitler in power, the 1936 Olympics in Berlin, Germany was marred by Aryan racism. Despite the pressure to perform, Owens went on to win four gold medals and set a new world record.

Upon his return to the United States, Owens was disappointed with the continuing discrimination experienced by blacks. To make matters worse, Owens had trouble finding work. He decided to turn professional, and began engaging in races against a horse, a car, and other nonhuman opponents. Professional racing, however, failed to materialize financially. In the 1940s, he pursued work on the lecture circuit, which proved to be more lucrative.

In 1972, while still working on the public speaking circuit, Owens moved to Phoenix, Arizona. He became a philanthropist. In Owens' name and with his financial support, the Jesse Owens Memorial Medical Center and the Jesse Owens Memorial Track Club was established. He also served on the boards of the National Council of Christians and Jews and the Boy Scouts of America. Owens died on March 31, 1980, in a Phoenix hospital.

BOOKER T. WASHINGTON
(Probably 1856 – November 14, 1915)

Occupation: educator, leader, social activist

Booker T. Washington, founder of the Tuskegee Normal and Industrial Institute, became one of the most controversial leaders of his time. At odds with W.E.B. Du Bois and other civil rights advocates, Washington was often called an accommodationist because he advocated self-help through economic means over civil and political rights.

Washington was born in western Virginia, probably in 1856. His father was an unknown white man, and his mother was the slave of James Burroughs. Washington worked as a house slave to the Burroughs family until 1865. After emancipation, Washington and his mother moved to Malden, West Virginia where her husband was working in the salt and coal mines.

Washington began working in the coalmine, and then in 1872 he enrolled at Hampton Normal and Agricultural Institute, which was run by Samuel Chapman Armstrong. After he graduated, he experimented with different options. He taught school in Malden, studied at a Baptist seminary, and worked in a lawyer's office. After trying his hand at various careers, Washington returned to Hampton where he settled into teaching for the next two years.

In 1881, Armstrong recommended him for the position of principal of a new black school, which was to be established in Tuskegee, Alabama. Washington was given the position, and with only two thousand dollars, he founded the Tuskegee Normal and Industrial Institute.

Tuskegee was an all-black school with an all-black faculty. Its teaching methods were modeled after the missionary method of Hampton. Emphasis was placed on self-determination, the skilled trades, and economic independence. Tuskegee also emphasized community. The Institute often bought surrounding farmland and sold it to small landowners and homeowners. By 1888, four hundred students were enrolled, and it owned five hundred acres of land.

Not long after the success of the school, Washington, "The Wizard of Tuskegee", garnered nationwide notoriety. He received national attention in 1895 when he made his speech, "The Atlanta Compromise", at the Cotton States and International Exposition. In his speech, he asserted that blacks and whites could remain separate in social matters, but in economic matters, there should not be any barriers to advancement. He also downgraded the importance of civil and political rights. In essence, Washington adopted a stance that appeared to tolerate segregation and discrimination.

After his address at the Exposition, whites and some blacks accepted Washington as a black leader. This new public position helped Washington promote and raise money for Tuskegee. Because of his views on race relations, Washington successfully entreated financial aid from wealthy whites and northern philanthropists. Shortly after 1895, Tuskegee was expanded nationwide. In 1900, Washington began another endeavor; he founded the National Negro Business League.

Washington was also a gifted speaker. In addition to speaking about the importance of economic self-sufficiency, he spoke about his opposition to universal suffrage, and believed that if enforced fairly, literacy and property tests should be used. He spoke separately to white and black audiences, and was able to appeal to both. To white audiences, he appealed to them by using black stereotypes, and often succeeded in gaining their support based on mutual interest, but not ideological agreement. To black audiences, he appealed to them by telling them not to cower to whites.

While Washington had a loyal following among some whites and blacks, his views were criticized by those in northern cities, southern black colleges, and educated black professionals who believed in political and civil rights, liberal education, and free expression. Critics called him many names such as Pope Washington, the Black Boss, The Benedict Arnold of the Negro Race, and the Great Traitor.

Critics such as William Monroe Trotter and W.E.B. Du Bois were among his most vocal opponents. Trotter, founder of the Boston Guardian, caused a stir in 1903 when he interrupted Washington's speech at a Boston Church. Trotter inundated Washington with questions that challenged his views, but his questions remained unanswered when Washington ignored him. Trotter was quickly arrested for disorderly conduct. The event was widely reported in newspapers, and became known as the "Boston Riot."

Another vocal critic, W.E. B. Du Bois, agreed with many of Trotter's criticism of Washington, and believed that Washington was misguided in his assertion that blacks should seek economic equality first. Du Bois instead asserted that economic security was not enough, and that blacks must become educated.

Although Washington publicly asserted that economic stability was most important, after his death when *The Booker T. Washington Papers* became public, it became known that he also tried to change lynching, disenfranchisement, and unequal facilities in education and transportation.

Among his several projects, Washington secretly worked with the National Afro-American Council on a court case that tested the constitutionality of a Louisiana grandfather clause. He funded the case with his own money and with the money of northern liberal white friends. Washington also had his lawyer secretly challenge an Alabama grandfather clause. It went to the U.S. Supreme Court, but lost on technicalities.

Washington also helped blacks who could not afford legal services. In one case, Washington got the criminal verdict against a black man overturned because blacks were excluded from the jury that had convicted him. In addition, Washington and two southern white attorneys got an Alabama peonage law declared unconstitutional after farm laborer, Alonzo Bailey, was held in peonage for debt.

After spending the latter part of his life serving as president of Tuskegee and as a black leader, on November 14, 1915, Washington died of arteriosclerosis at St. Luke's Hospital in New York.

While Washington's views and priority of economic self-sufficiency over civil and political rights were controversial, Washington created a successful educational institution that is still in existence today and has become the degree granting college, Tuskegee University.

MALCOLM X
(May 19, 1925 – February 21, 1965)

Occupation: civil rights leader

Malcolm X was initially known for his controversial stance of racial separatism, but after his pilgrimage to Mecca, while he still advocated Black Nationalism, he also accepted a more orthodox Islam view of the "true brotherhood" of man. He came to believe that there was a potential for cross-racial alliance.

Named Malcolm Little by his parents, Malcolm X was born on May 19, 1925, in Omaha, Nebraska. Malcolm's father, Earl Little, was an outspoken supporter of the Black Nationalist Marcus Garvey. As a result, he received numerous death threats and was forced to move his family several times.

While the family was in Lansing, Michigan, their home was burned down. Two years later, Malcolm's father was murdered. Malcolm's mother had an emotional breakdown and was unable to care for Malcolm and his siblings. The children were split up and sent to foster homes.

By the time that Malcolm was a teenager, he had dropped out of high school. At first, he worked odd jobs in Boston, Massachusetts, but he soon moved to Harlem, New York and became involved in criminal activity. Malcolm moved back to Boston, and shortly thereafter, he was convicted of burglary in 1946.

While Malcolm was in prison, he converted to the Muslim religious sect, the Nation of Islam. When he was released in

1952, he changed his last name to X because he considered the name "Little" to have been a slave name. The Nation of Islam's leader, Elijah Muhammad, made Malcolm a minister and sent him around the country on speaking engagements. Malcolm spoke about black pride and separatism, and rejected the civil rights movement's focus on integration and equality.

Malcolm was a charismatic speaker, and soon was able to use newspaper columns, television, and radio to spread the Nation of Islam's message. Membership to the Nation of Islam increased dramatically because of Malcolm's speeches. However, while many blacks were embracing his message, civil rights leaders rejected him. Malcolm also became a concern of the government. The Federal Bureau of Investigation began surveillance of him and infiltrated the Nation of Islam.

While Malcolm had garnered increasing attention, his relationship with Elijah Muhammad became strained in 1963. Malcolm learned that, contrary to Muhammad's teaching of celibacy until marriage, Muhammad was having sexual relations with six women. Malcolm felt that Muhammad was committing fraud, and he refused to keep it a secret.

Malcolm X's relationship with Muhammad became even more strained when he made some controversial statements. When President John F. Kennedy was assassinated on November 22, 1963, Malcolm publicly described it as "the chickens coming home to roost". Because of this comment, Muhammad silenced him for ninety days.

In March 1964, Malcolm left the Nation of Islam and founded the Muslim Mosque, Inc. A month later, he took a pilgrimage to Mecca, Saudi Arabia. It was there that his view of separatism changed. He discovered that white and black Muslims could coexist together. While he still advocated Black Nationalism, he also accepted a more orthodox Islam view of the "true brotherhood" of man and believed that there was a potential for cross-racial alliance.

When he returned to the United States, he stopped advocating separatism, and instead relayed the message of integration and world brotherhood. However, he discovered that the Nation of Islam wanted to assassinate him. On February 14, 1965, his home was firebombed, but no one was hurt.

A few days later on February 21, 1965, while Malcolm was on stage at the Manhattan Audubon Ballroom, three gunmen shot him to death. The gunmen were arrested and convicted. It was later discovered that they were members of the Nation of Islam. Malcolm was buried on February 27, 1965, in Hartsdale, New York.

Since his death, his popularity has continued, and is partly due to the publication of *The Autobiography of Malcolm X* and Spike Lee's 1992 movie, *Malcolm X*.

Appendix 5

Selecting a Male Role Model

Carefully select a man to model your life after. Find someone you respect and admire.

Describe his strengths.

_____
_____
_____
_____
_____
_____
_____

Why did you select him?

_____
_____
_____
_____
_____
_____
_____

Describe his uplifting and inspiring qualities:

_____
_____
_____
_____
_____
_____

Appendix 6

Understanding Oppression

It is important to understand oppression. Some of you are suffering from oppression and do not know it. You accept oppressive views and negative stereotypes that hinder your ability to progress productively. The first step to conquer internalized oppression is to understand what it is. Knowing is half the battle. I hope you find this information to be helpful.

Psychological Manifestation of Internalized Oppression

- Feels inferior (constantly trying to prove your manhood or ability to perform to others standards) overcompensating for educational, environmental, and personal shortcomings, i.e., bragging, lying about accomplishments, belittling others, etc.
- Feels powerless and helpless (give up easily; exhibiting self-destructive and self-inhibiting attitudes: "I don't care"; "things will never change", etc.)
- Strong willed or stubborn (don't ask for help, difficulty acknowledging faults, etc.)
- Have to be in control (refuse or afraid to show weakness or vulnerability)
- Distrustful (everybody is out to hurt you)
- Emotionally reserved and restricted (lacks ability to share emotions)
- Low self-esteem or self-doubt (view self in a subordinate manner; lacks confidence, etc.)

Behavioral Manifestation of Internalized Oppression

- Attempt to control others
- Competitive attitude; strives to dominate those who are perceived to be weaker
- Degrade others
- Withdraws from others
- Difficulty accepting or asking for help
- Use sexuality and doing to demonstrate affection
- Uses force, intimidation, or violence to get needs met

Common Characteristics of males suffering from Internalized Oppression

- Has low self-esteem
- Believes all the myths about battering relationships
- Is a traditionalist
- Blames others for his actions
- Is pathologically jealous
- Presents a dual personality
- Has severe stress reactions
- Uses sex as an act of aggression
- Does not believe violent behavior should have negative consequences

Appendix 7

Positive Self-Concept Screening Questionnaire

If you answer no to one or more of the questions below, please talk to someone who can help you understand your emotions. It is important to seek support and understanding to prevent depression or other mental health challenges.

Do you strive to do your best and feel good about yourself regardless of the outcome? Yes or No

Do you think highly of yourself? Yes or No

Do you engage in self-praise? Yes or No

Do you try new things without fear of being teased or failing? Yes or No

Do you believe you are equal to others? Yes or No

Do you have high confidence? Yes or No

Do you express yourself positively when people demean, disrespect or belittle you? Yes or No

Do you feel good about yourself? Yes or No

Do you feel hopeful? Yes or No

Do you feel that you are worthy of praise from others? Yes or No

Appendix 8

Strength Inventory

List at least nine personal strengths and practice them daily to help you conquer oppression and improve your self-esteem.

1.) _____
2.) _____
3.) _____
4.) _____
5.) _____
6.) _____
7.) _____
8.) _____
9.) _____

Learn to focus on your strengths for inspiration. Resiliency is achieved by demonstrating the ability to move forward after experiencing sustained or prolonged trauma or difficulty.

Note Page

_____
_____
_____
_____
_____
_____
_____
_____
_____
_____
_____
_____
_____
_____
_____
_____
_____
_____
_____
_____
_____
_____
_____
_____
_____

Note Page

_____
_____
_____
_____
_____
_____
_____
_____
_____
_____
_____
_____
_____
_____
_____
_____
_____
_____
_____
_____
_____
_____
_____
_____
_____
_____
_____
_____
_____
_____
_____
_____

Scheduling For Seminars, Speaking Engagements or Film Screenings

Dr. Buckingham conducts seminars, speaking engagements and film screenings for groups, churches, and organizations throughout the year.

"A Black Man's Worth" is one of the most requested seminars; however, Dr. Buckingham conducts seminars and speaks on a variety of topics related to relationship difficulty, stress management, team building and personal growth.

RHCS is dedicated to expanding the horizons of all humans!

To book Dr. Buckingham for your next event:

R.E.A.L. Horizons Consulting Service, LLC
P.O. Box 2665
Silver Spring, MD 20915

240-242-4087 Voice Mail
www.realhorizonsdlb.com

I hope this book has been a blessing to you and I welcome your comments.
dwayne@realhorizonsdlb.com

This book can also be purchased online at:

www.realhorizonsdlb.com

Amazon.com

Borders.com

BarnesandNoble.com

BooksaMillion.com

About the Author

Dwayne L. Buckingham, Ph.D., LCSW, BCD, is a psychotherapist, film producer and the Founder and Chief Executive Officer of R.E.A.L. Horizons Consulting Service, LLC in Silver Spring, Maryland. A commissioned officer in the United States Air Force, for nearly a decade he provided psychological assessments and treatment to over ten thousand individuals, couples, groups, and families worldwide. Dr. Buckingham currently serves as a Commander in the United States Public Health Service and provides individual and marital therapy to military troops assigned to the Walter Reed National Military Medical Center in Bethesda, Maryland. Also, he is an active member of the National Association of Social Workers and Kappa Alpha Psi Fraternity, Inc. Dr. Buckingham conducts educational wellness seminars for individuals, groups, families, organizations, and churches each year. Please visit his Website at www.realhorizonsdlb.com for more information.